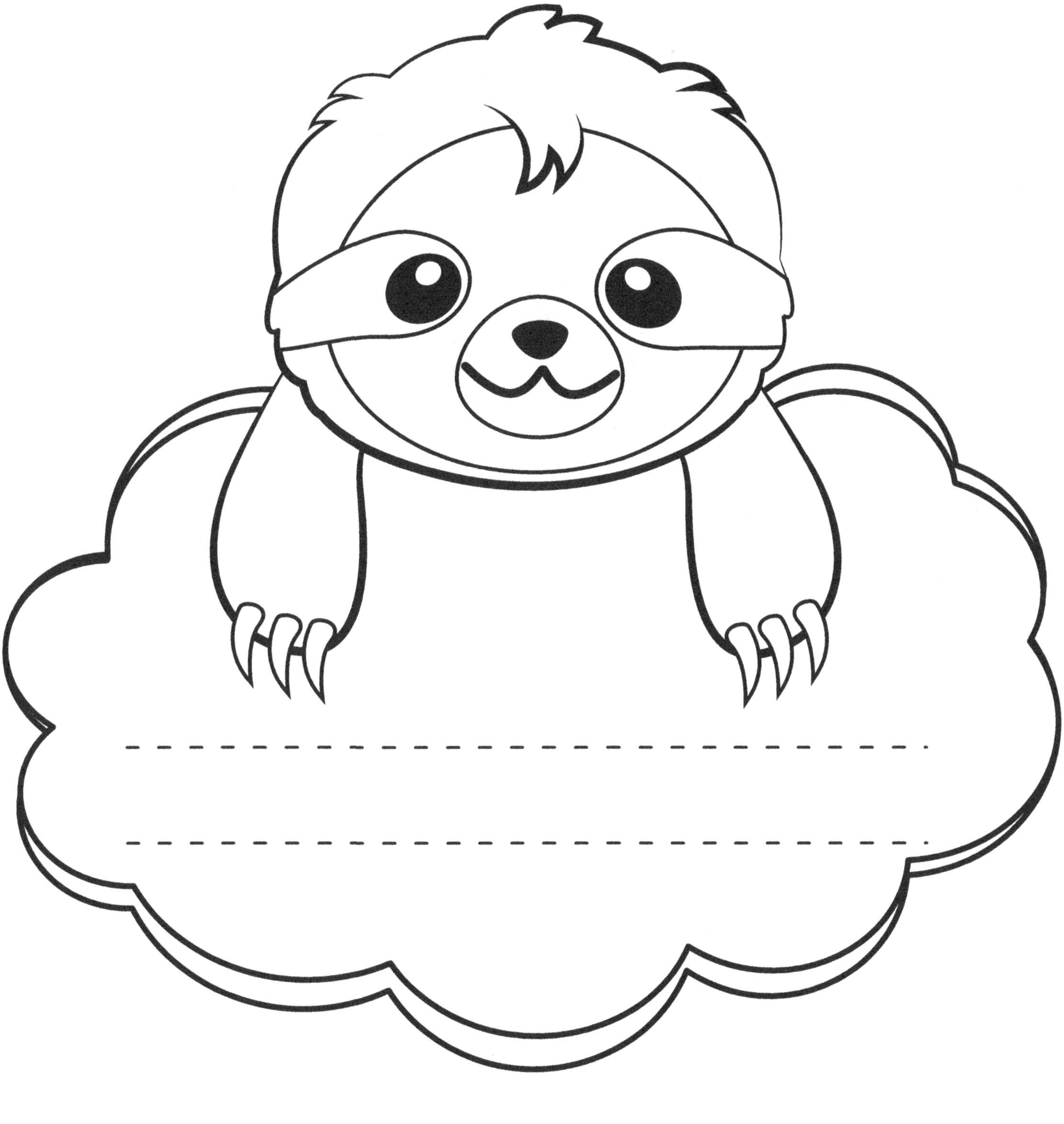

FARTING SLOTH

COLORING BOOK

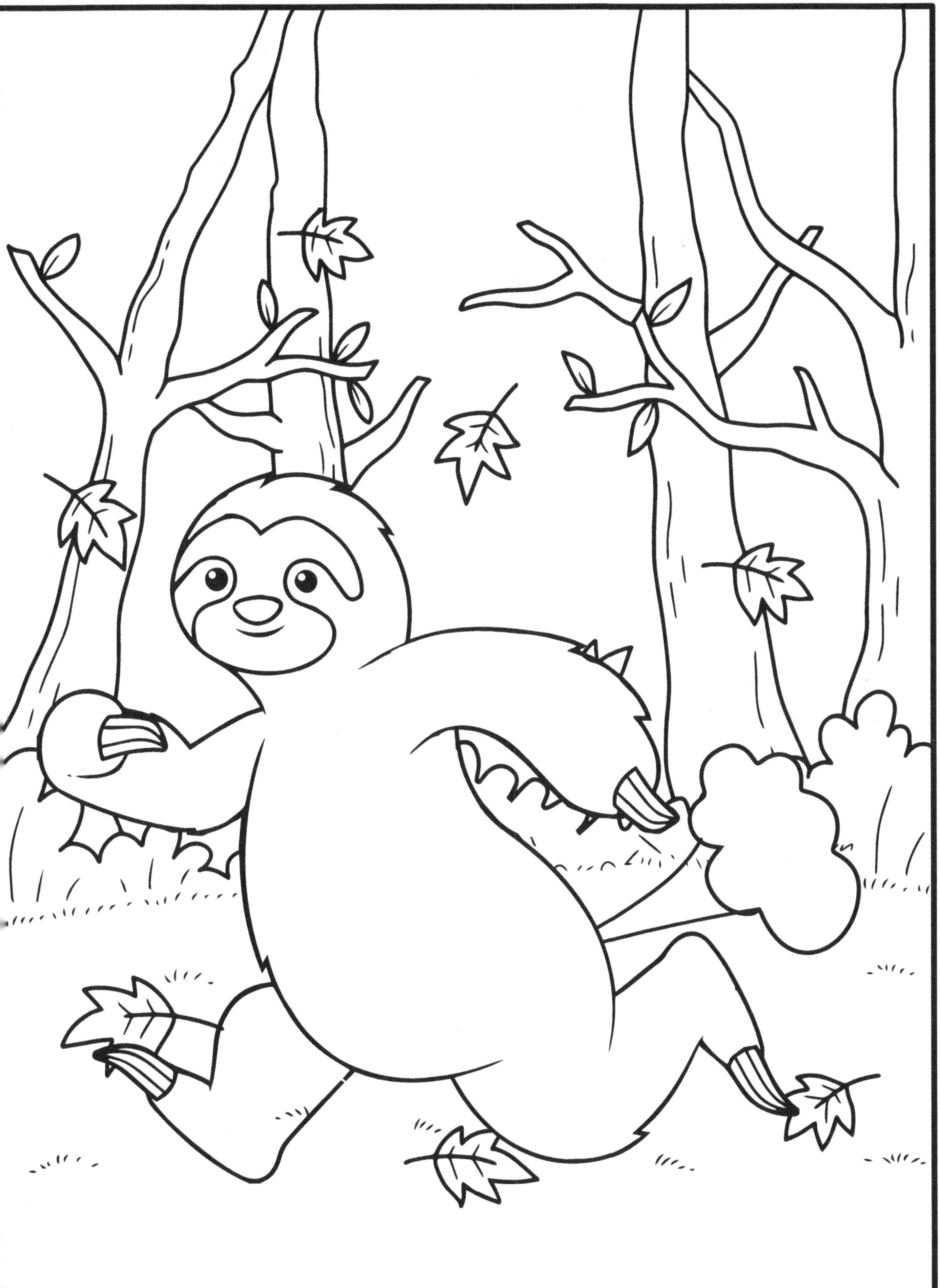

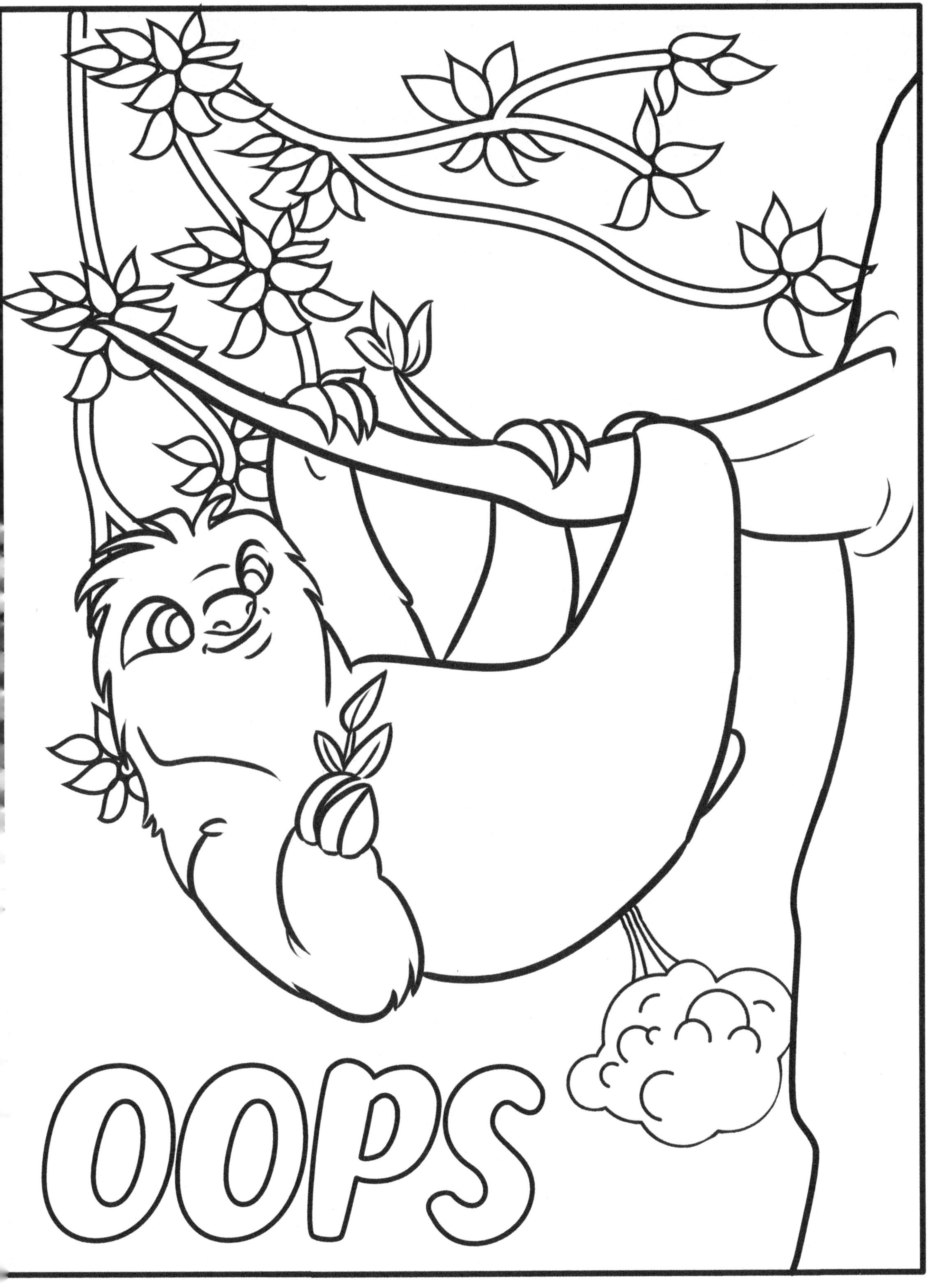
OOPS

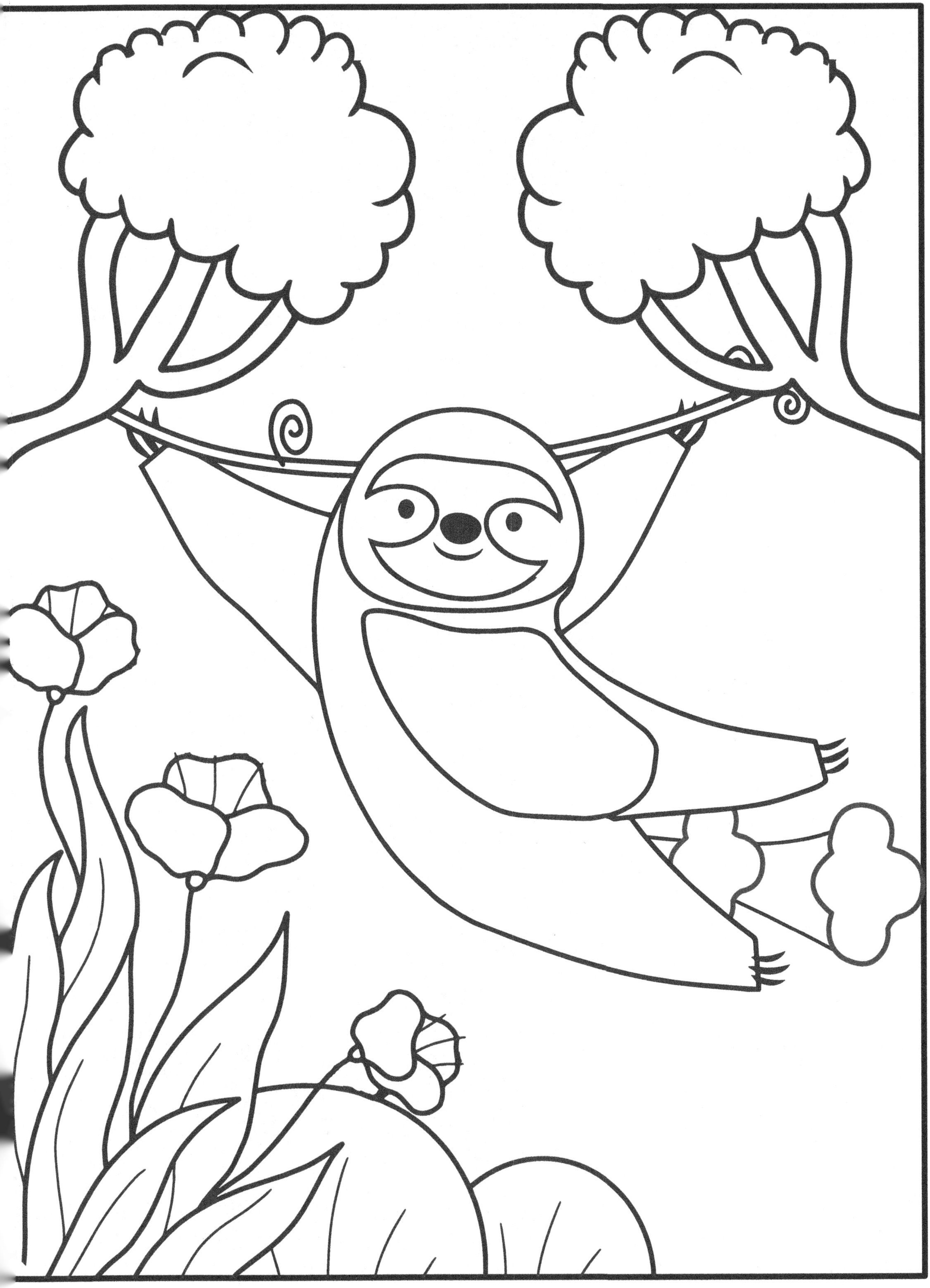

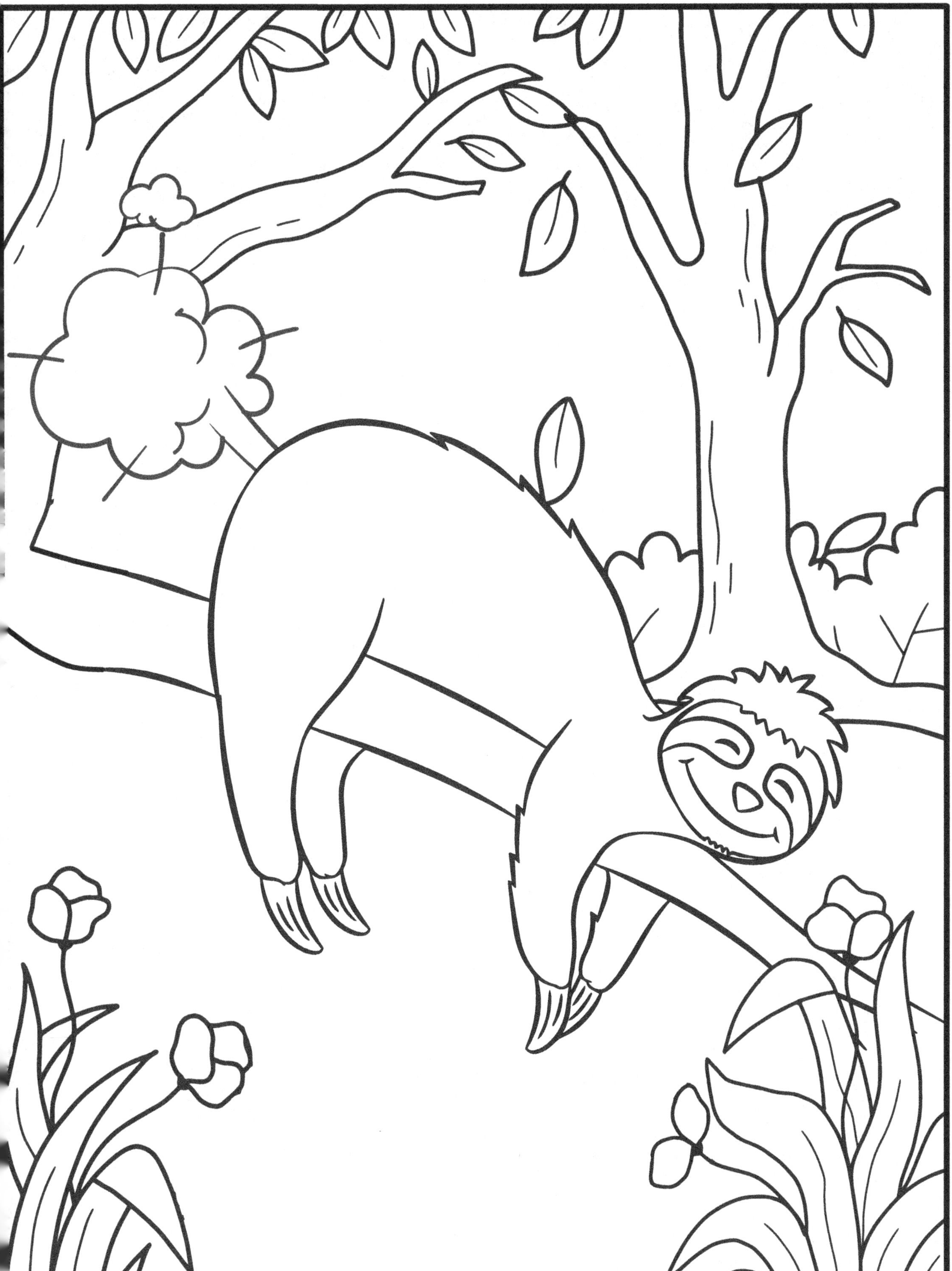

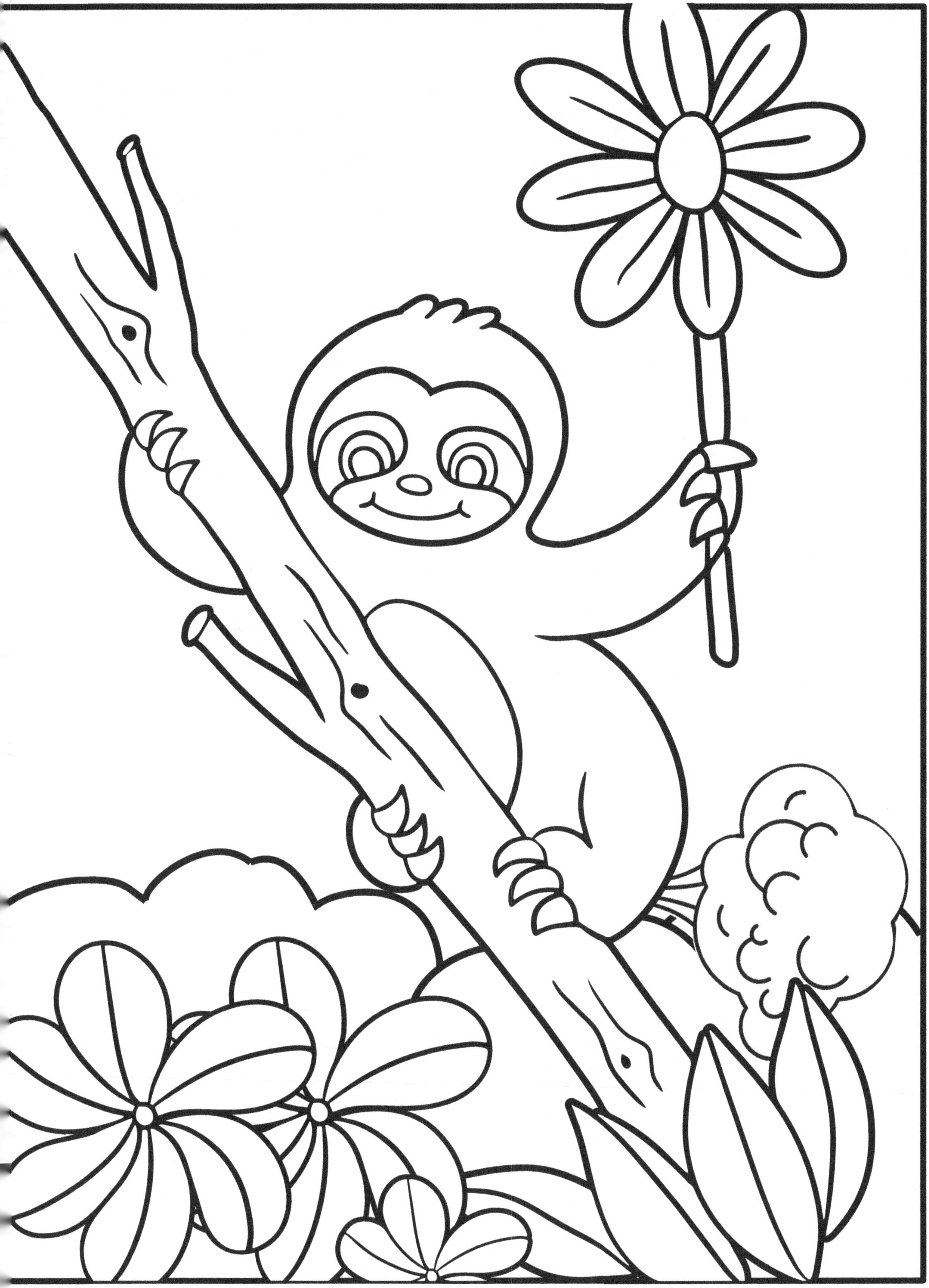

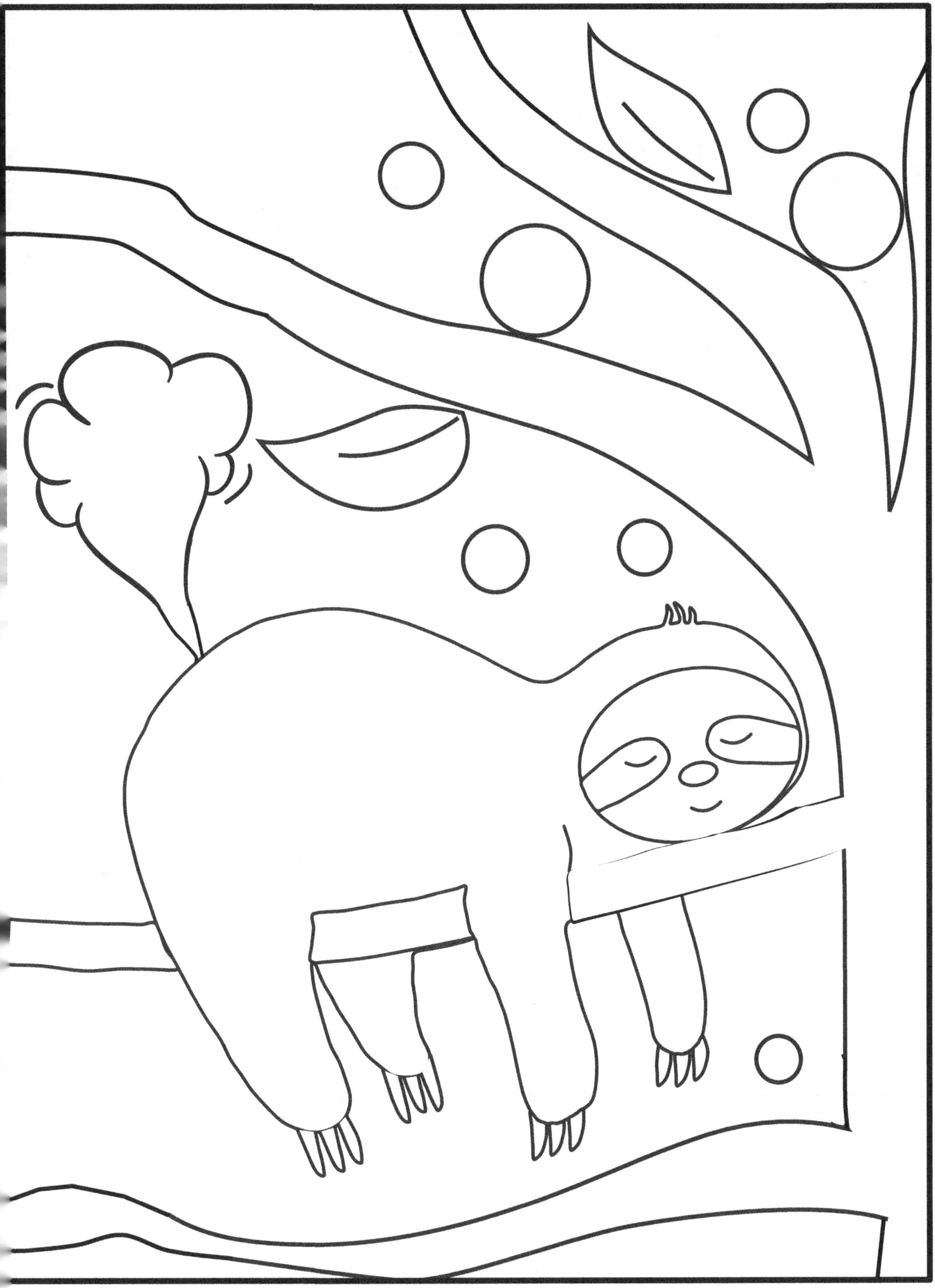

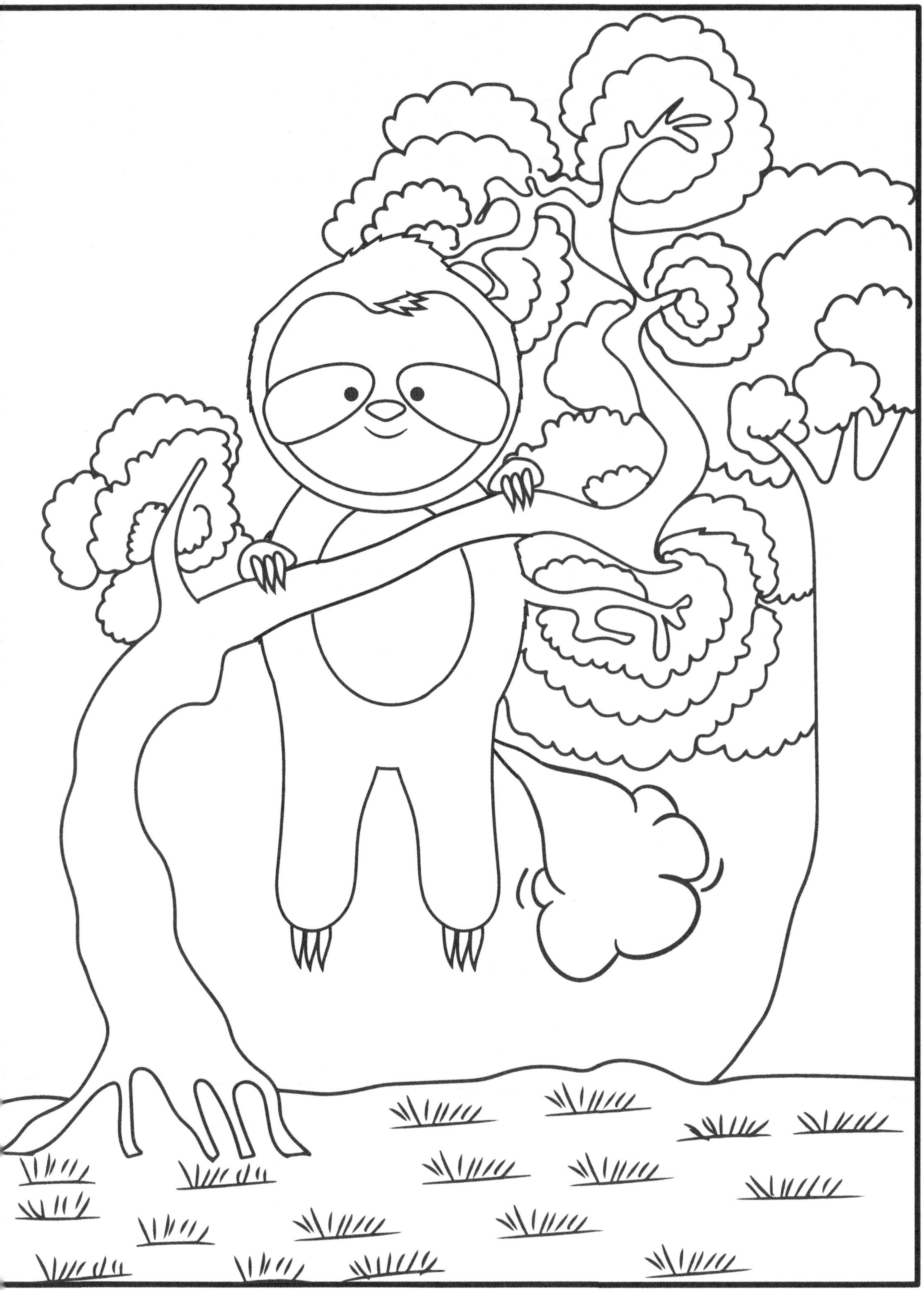

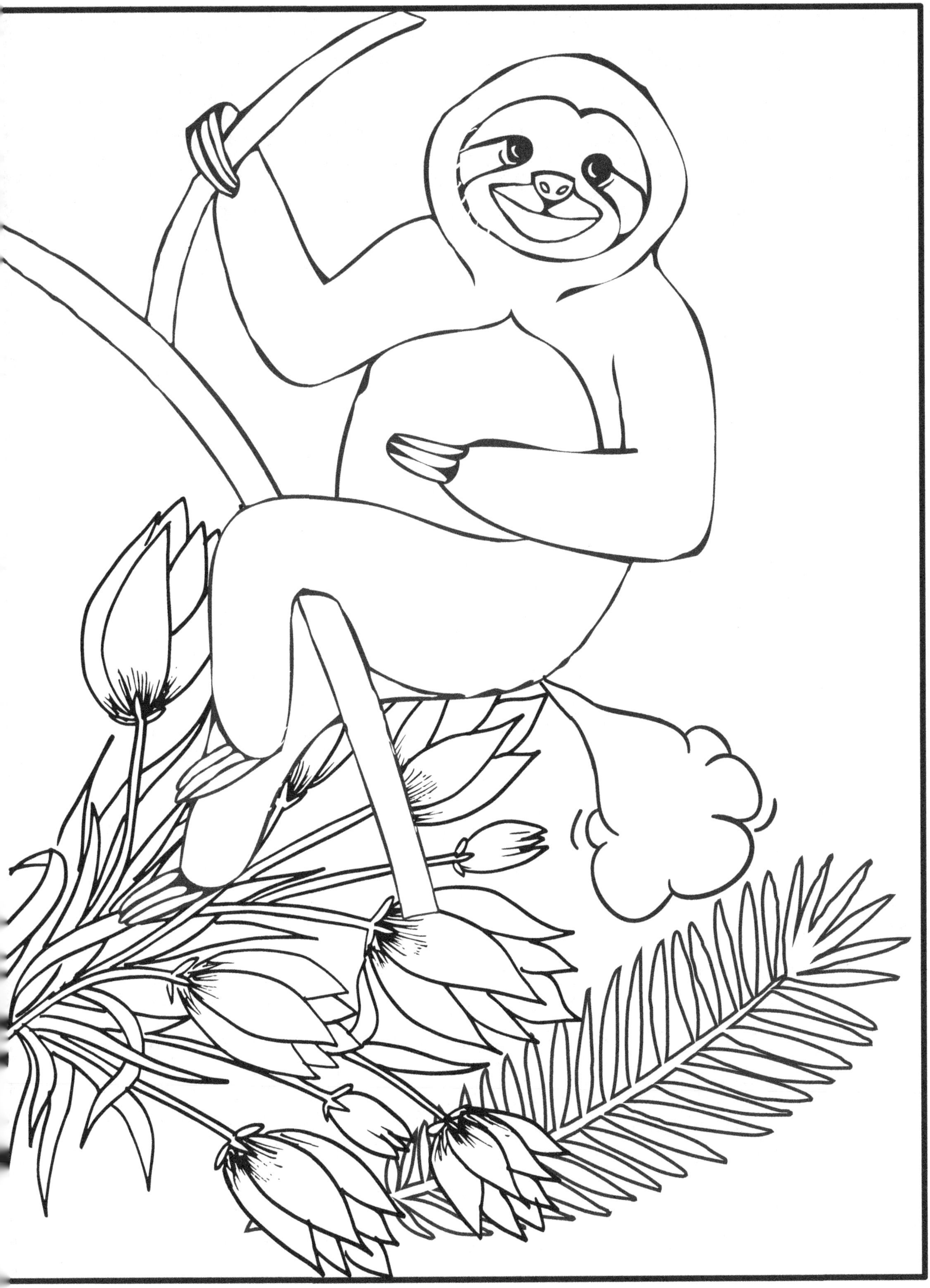

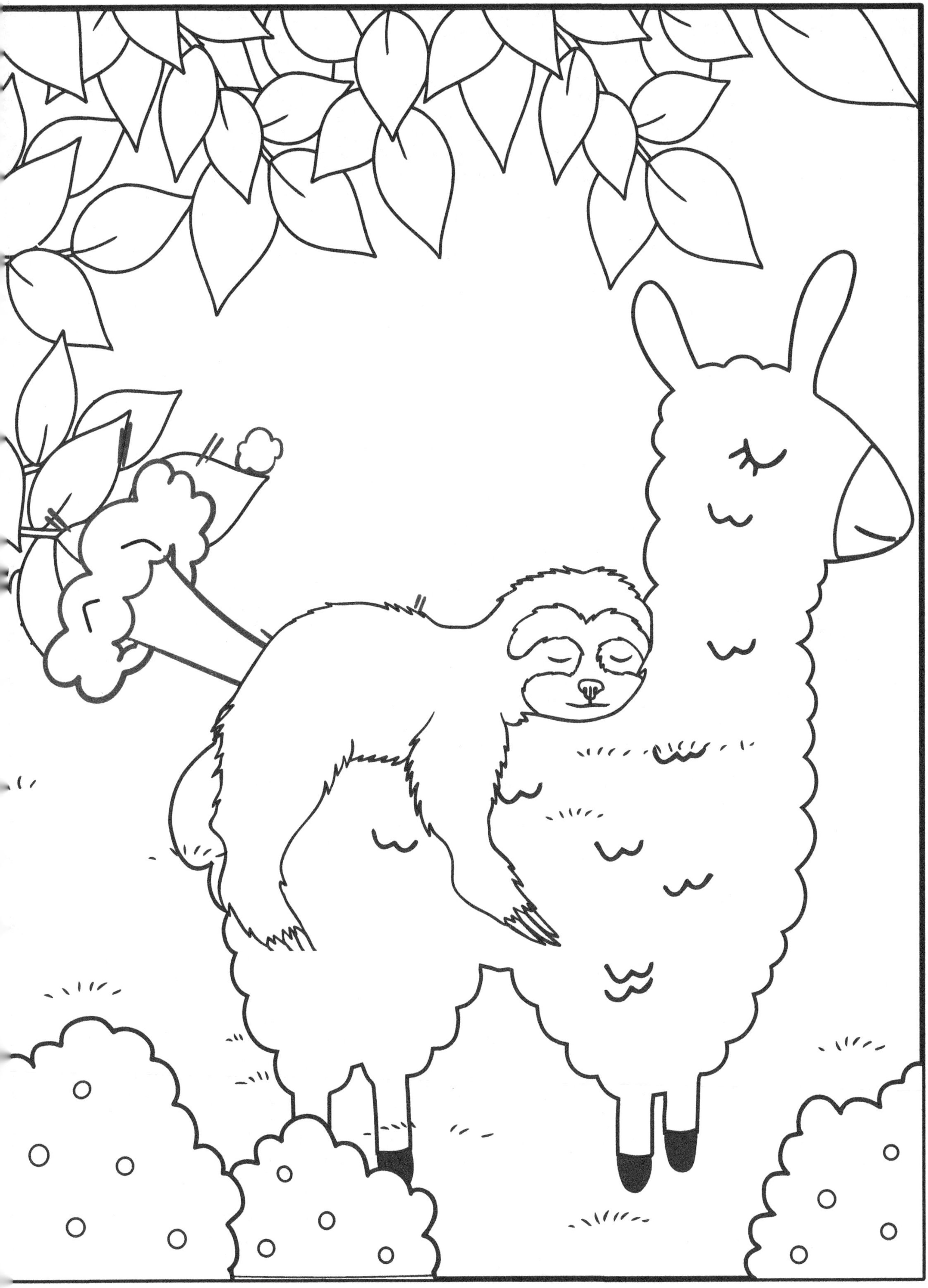

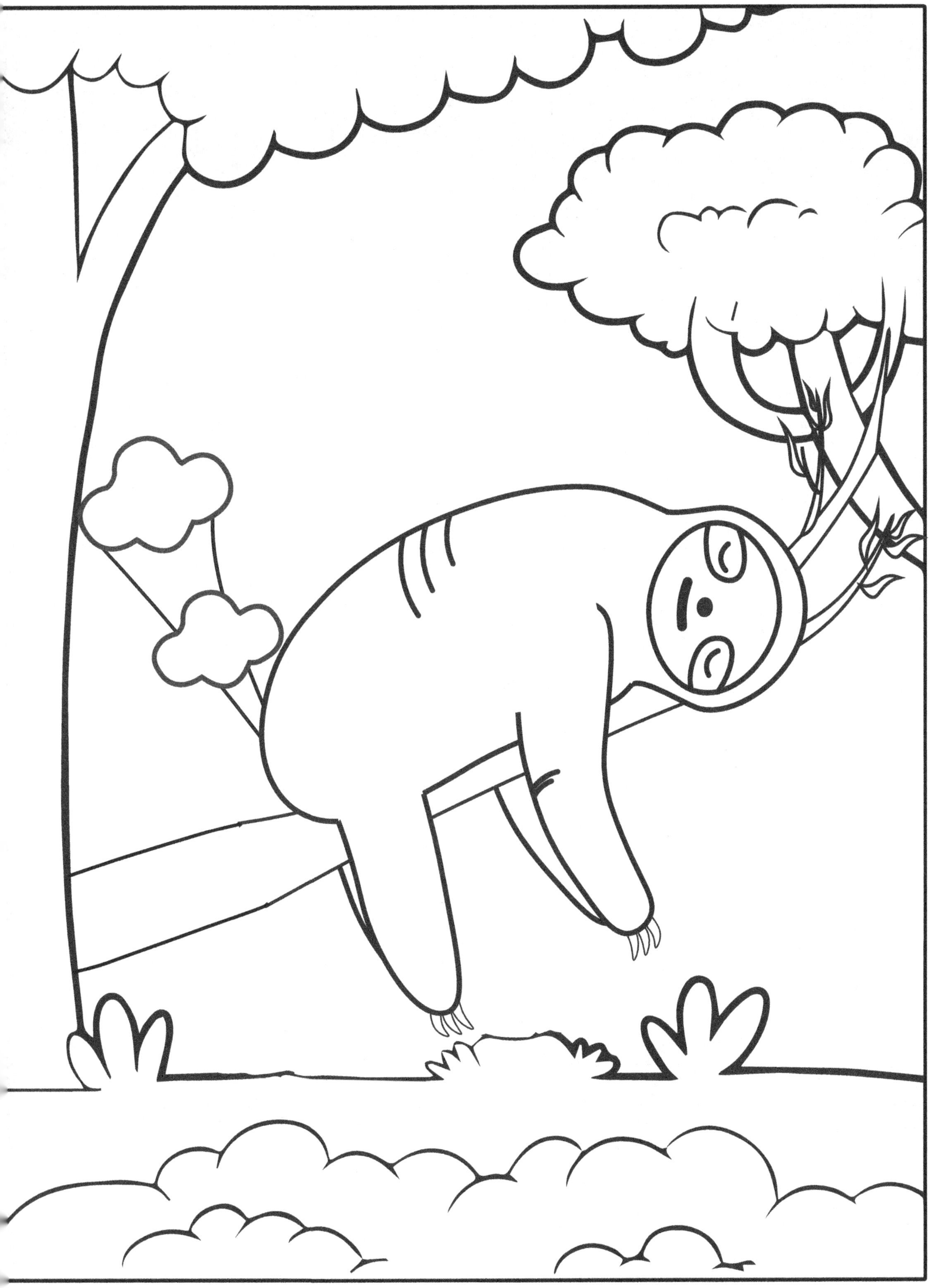

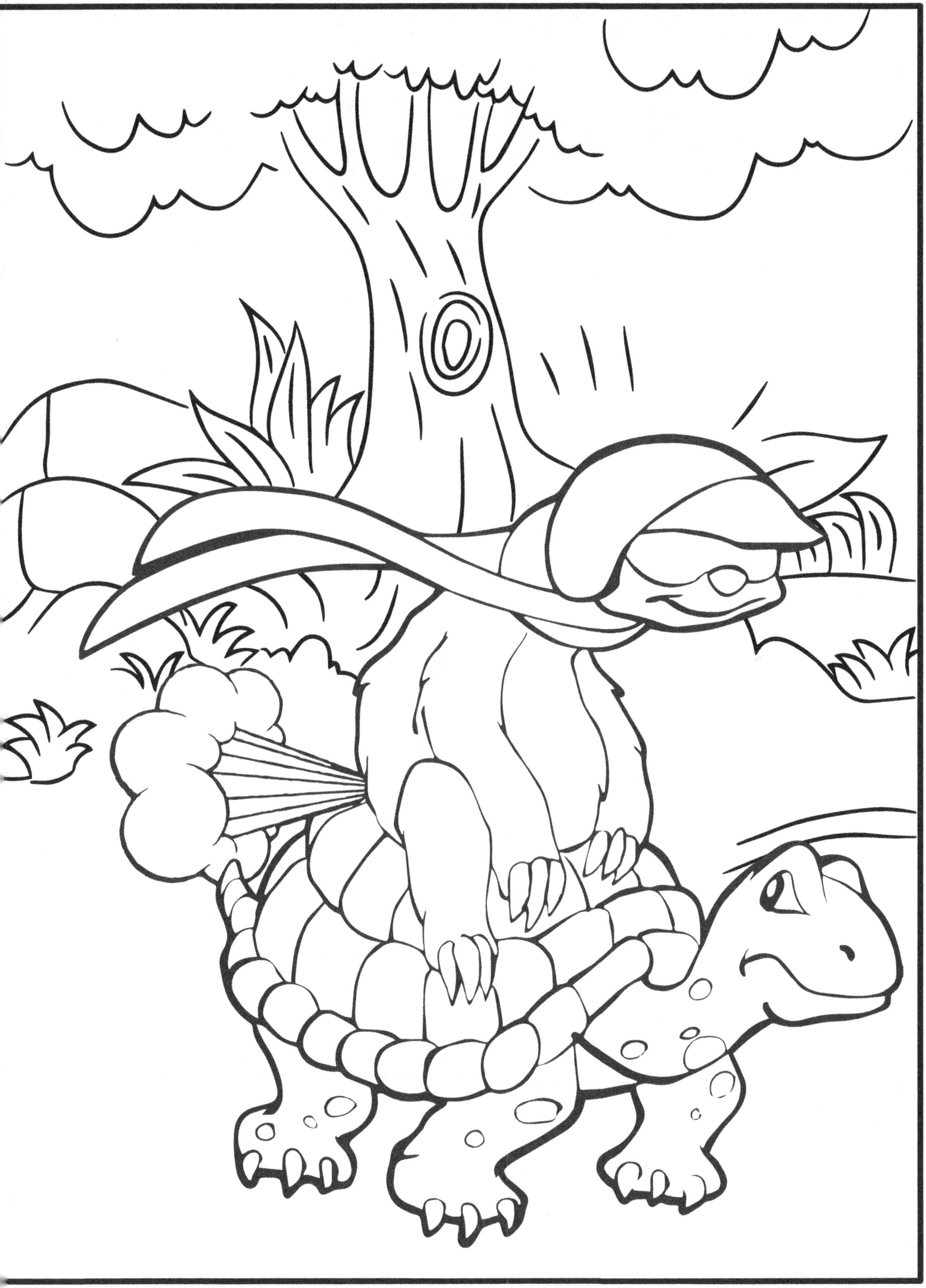

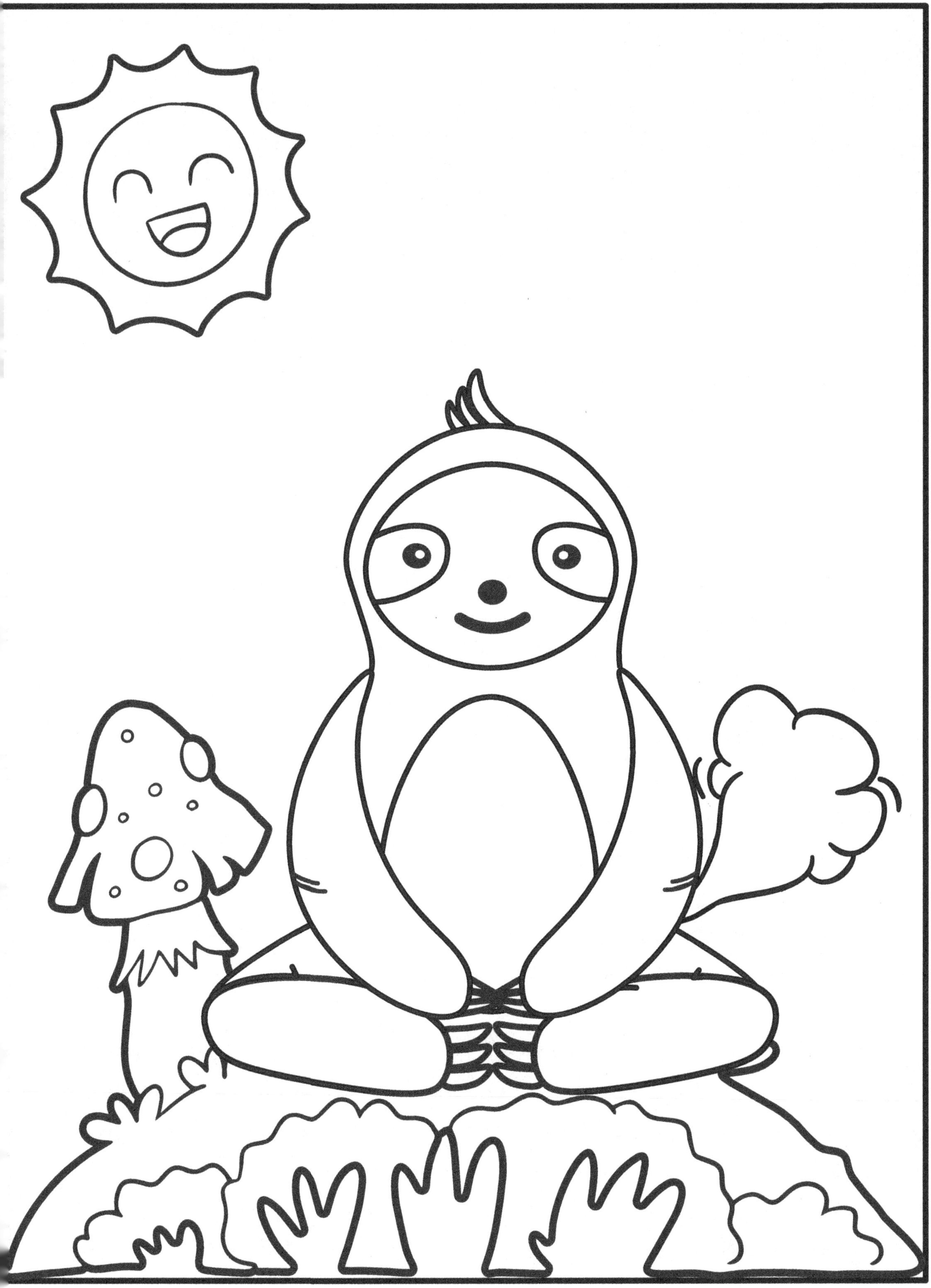

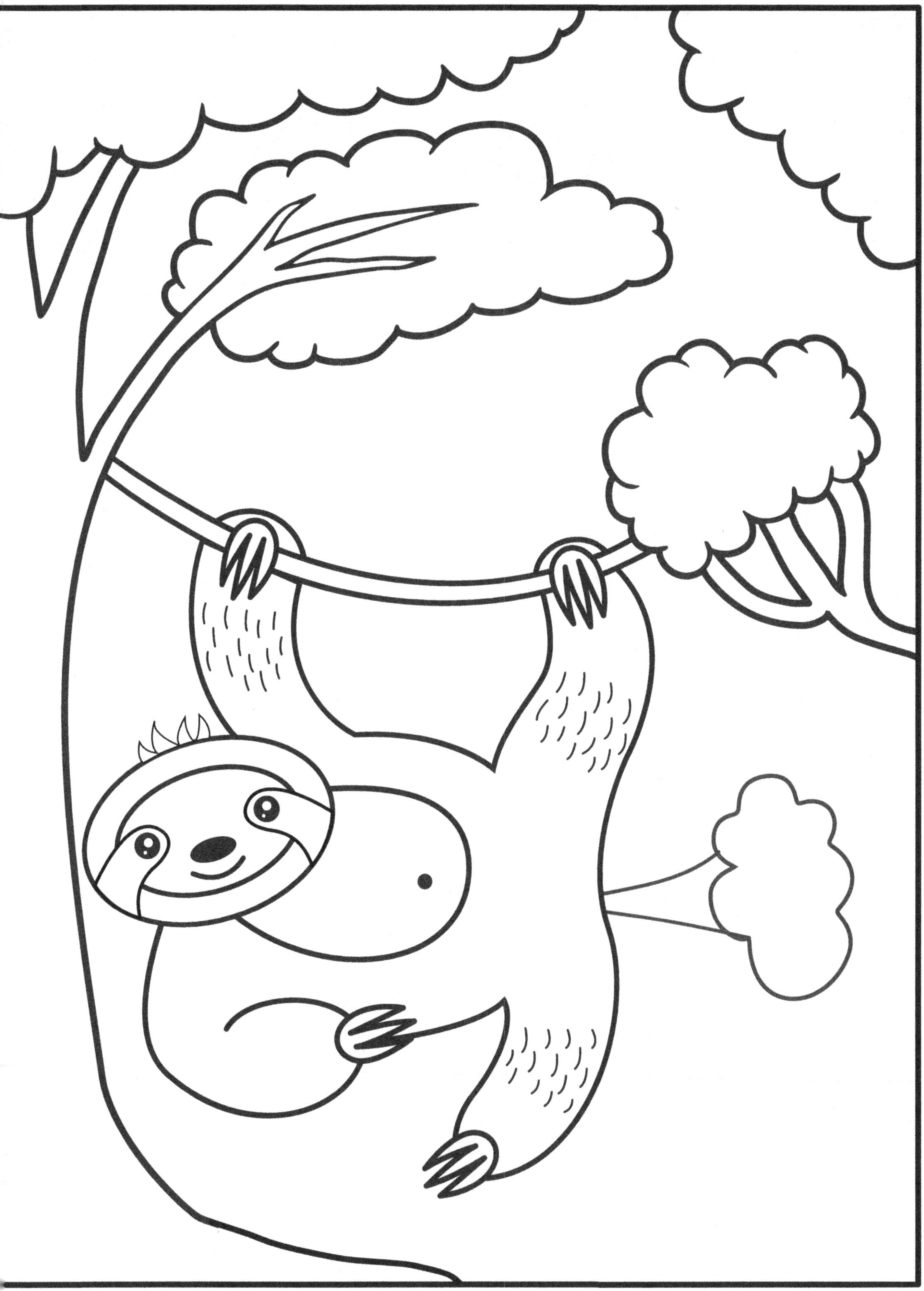

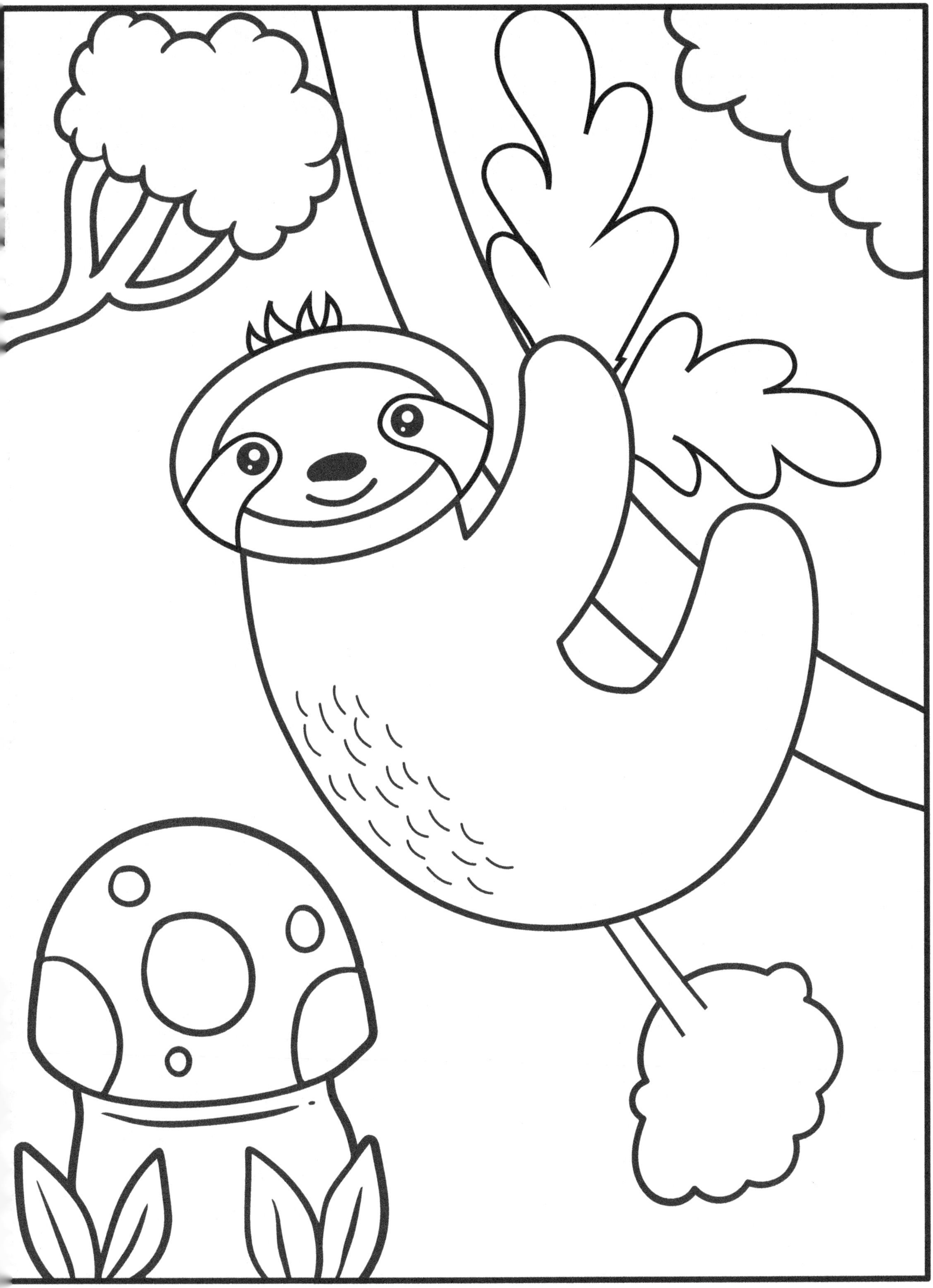

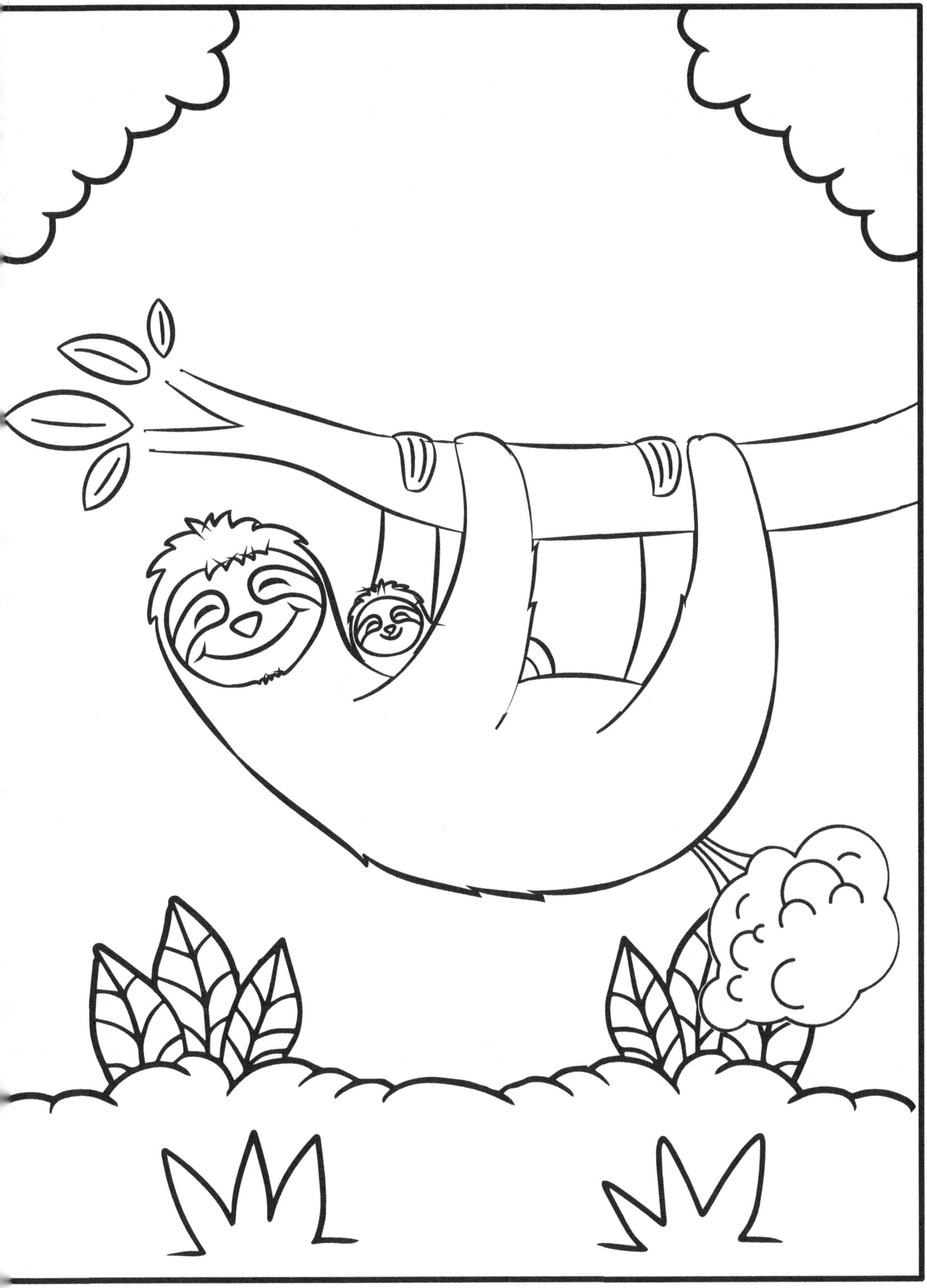

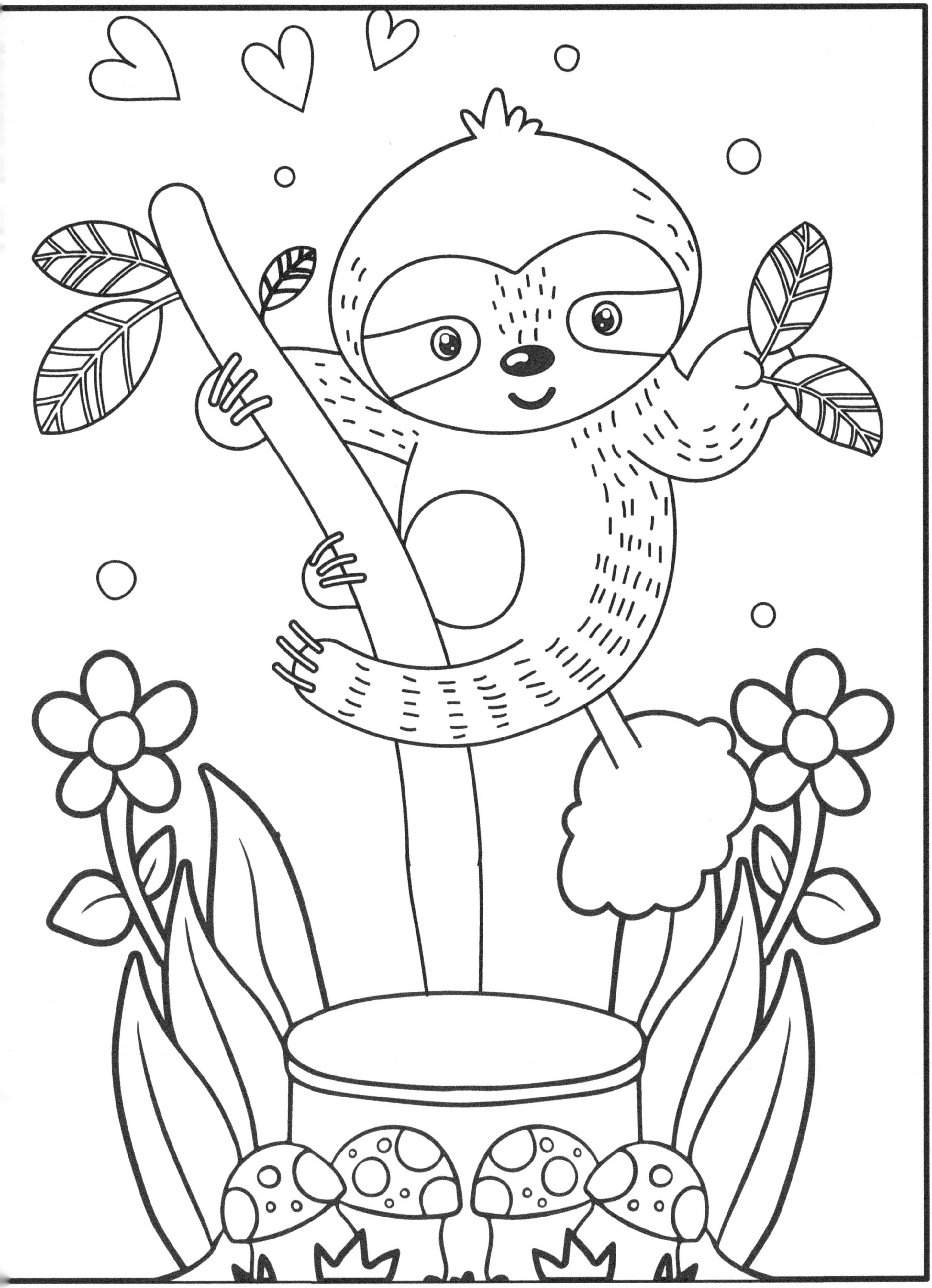

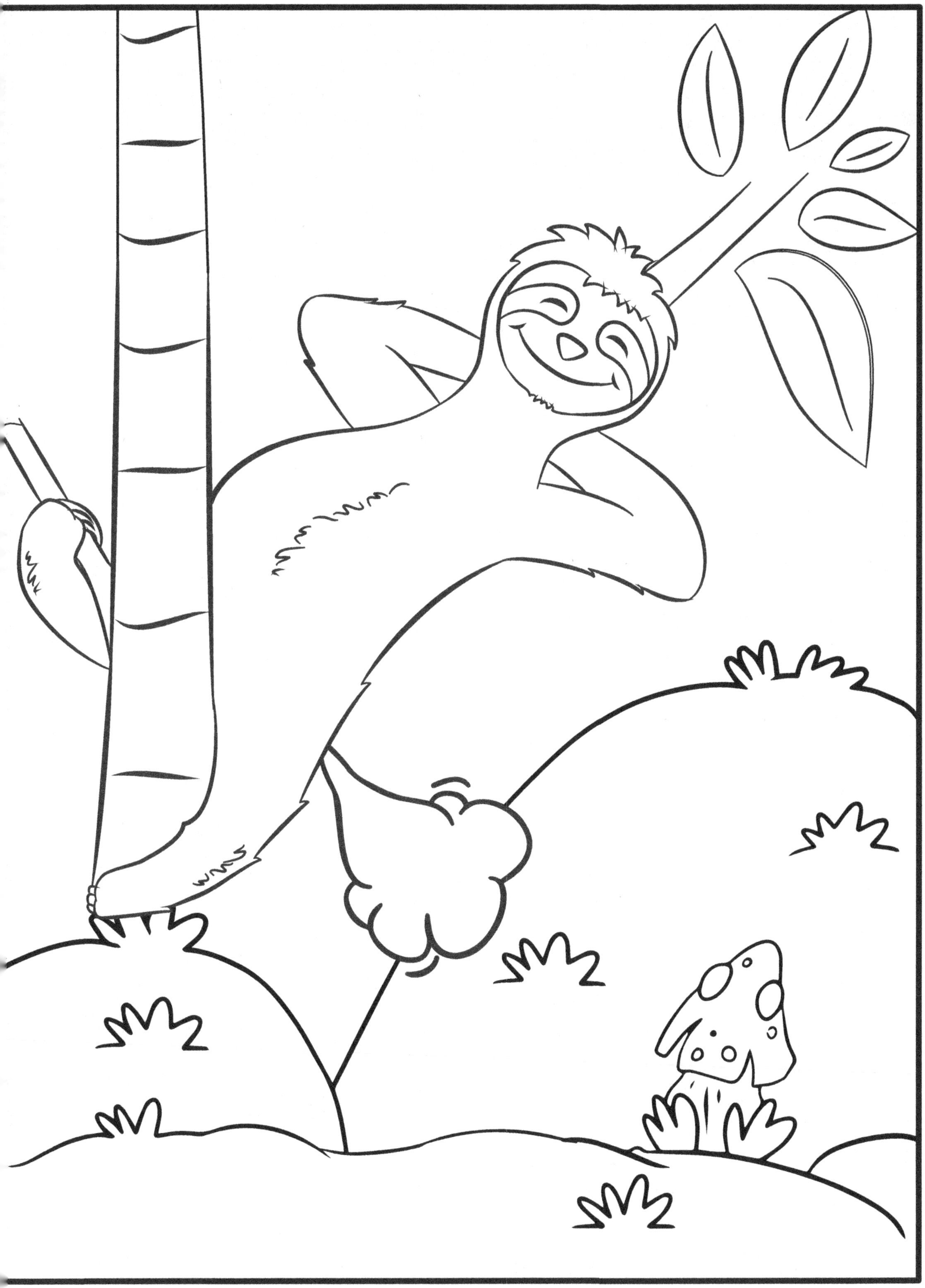

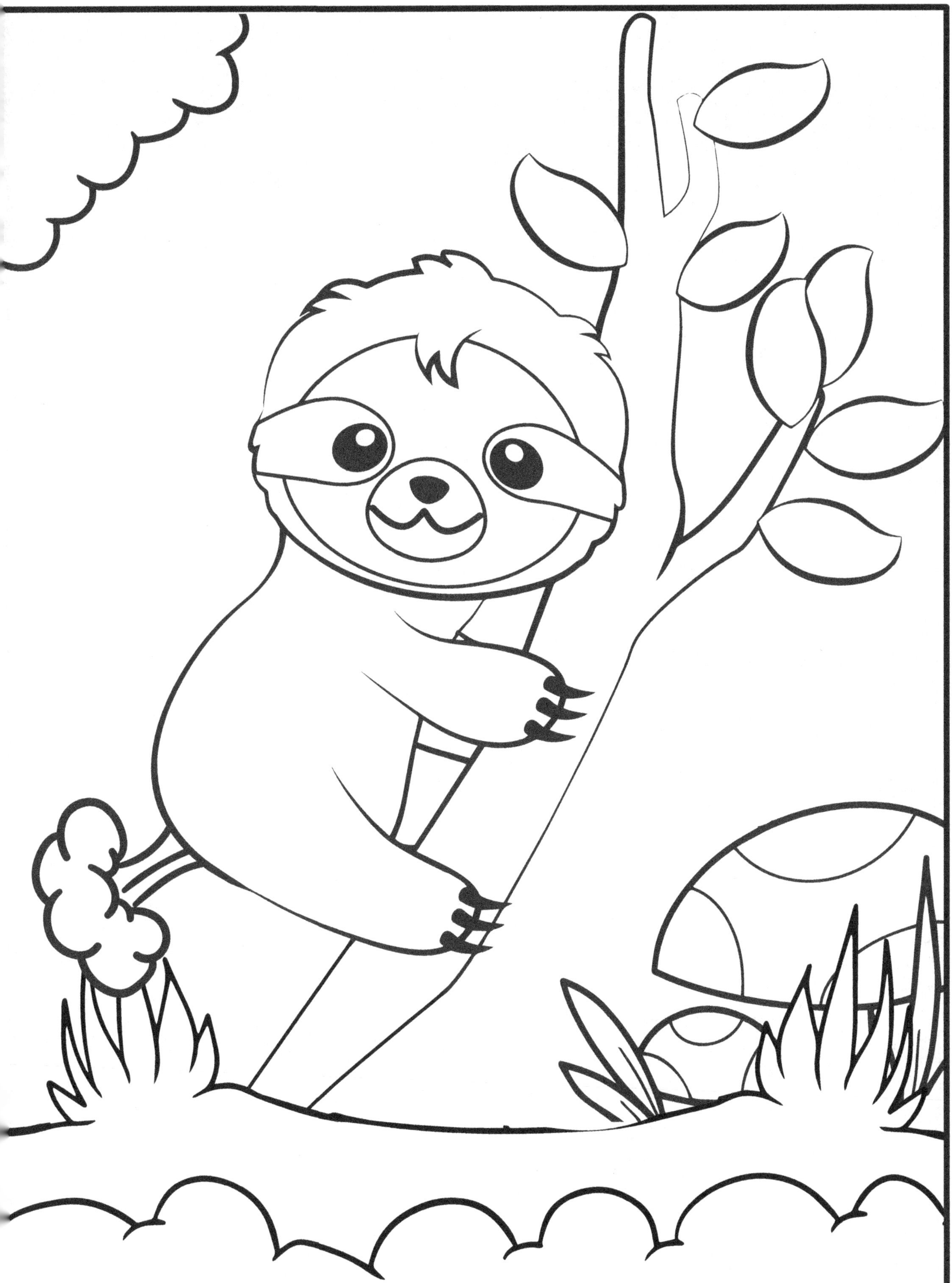

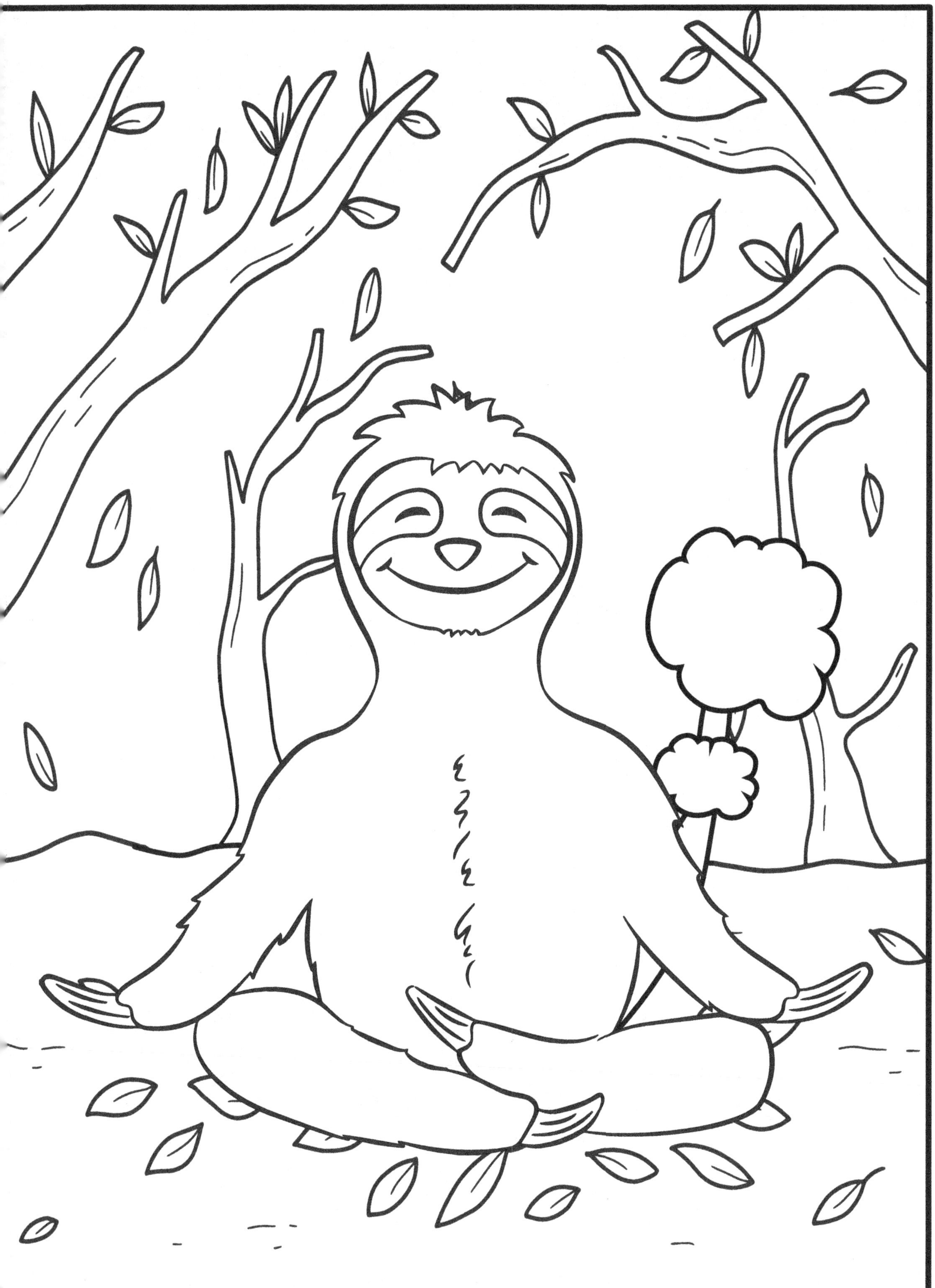

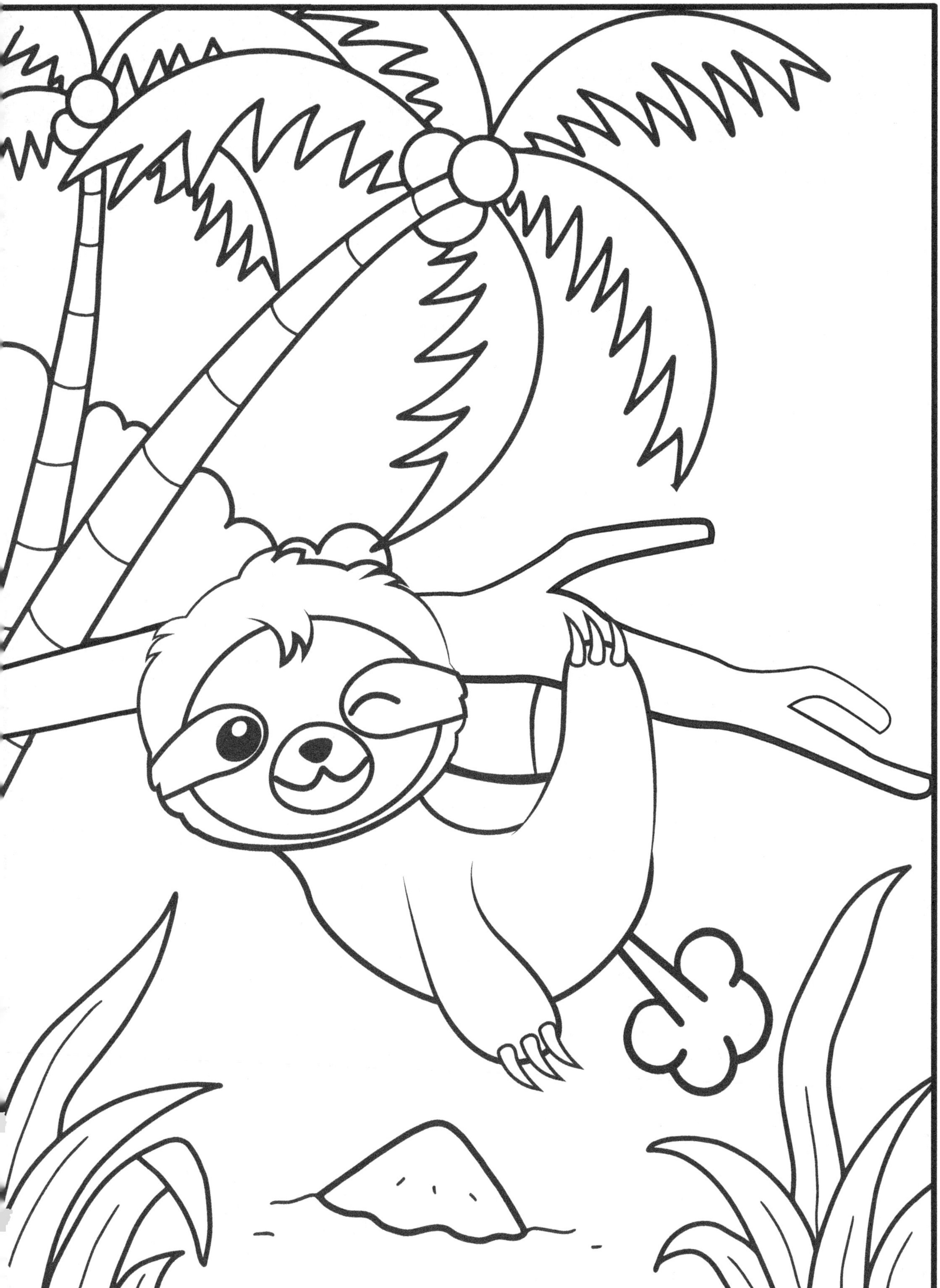

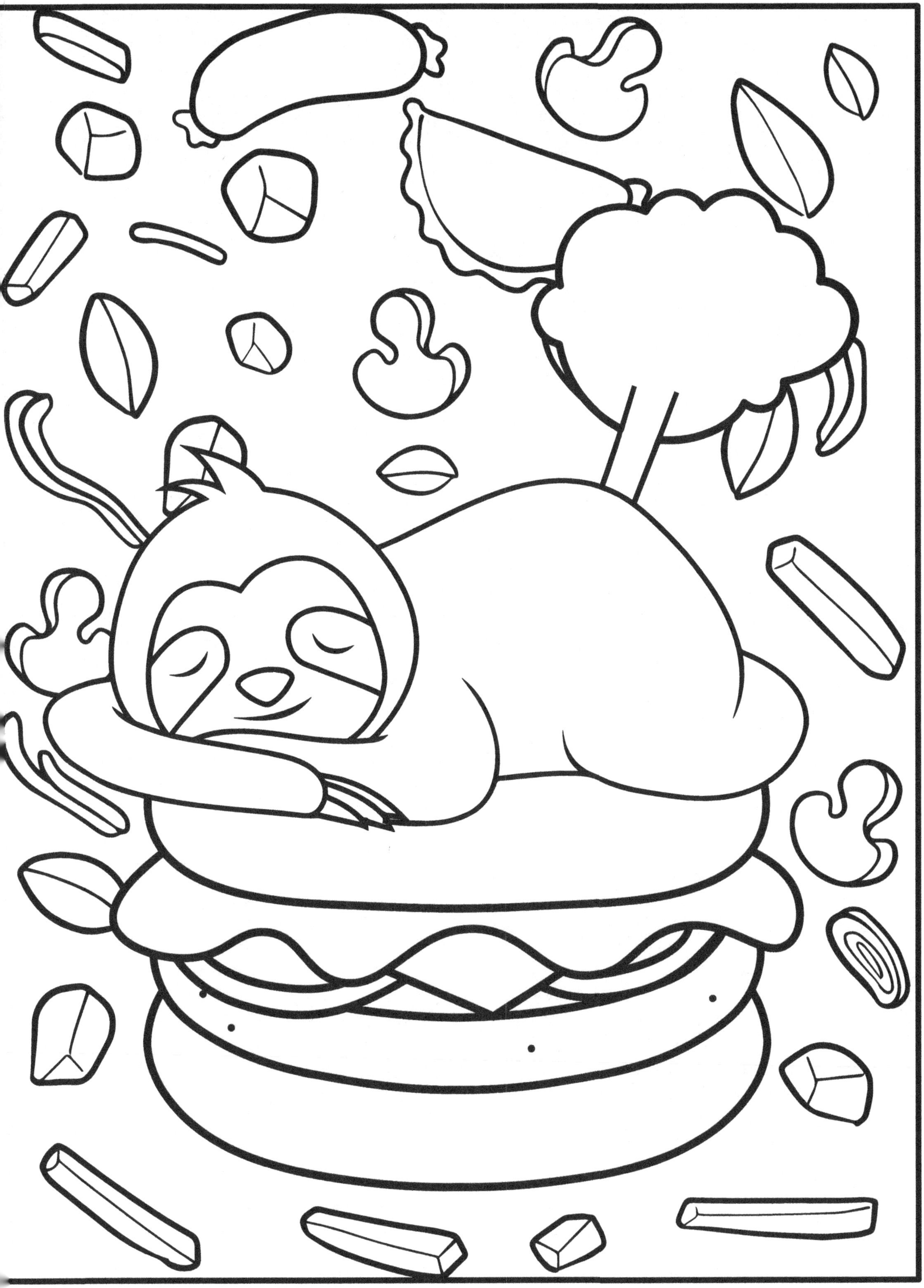

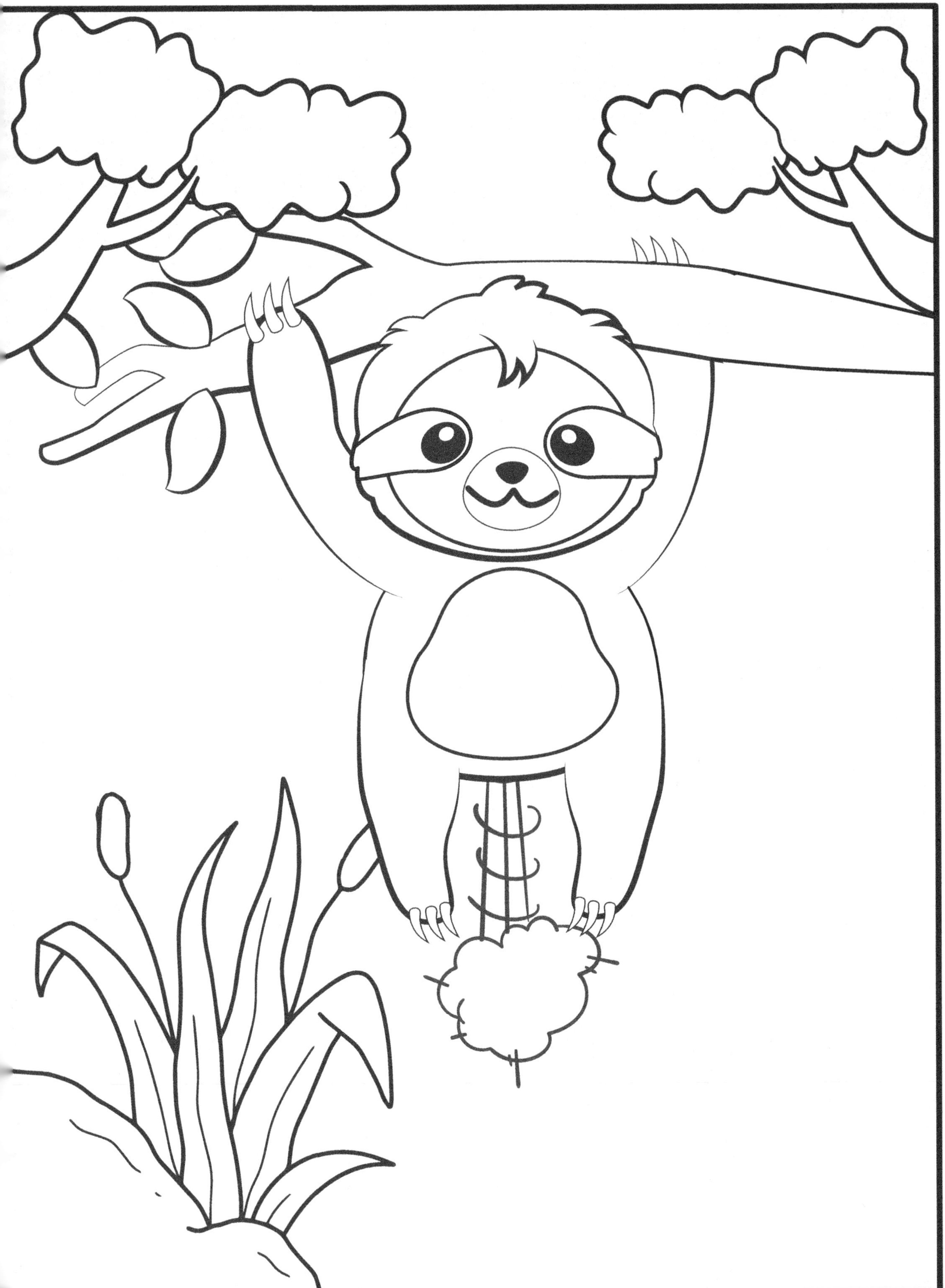

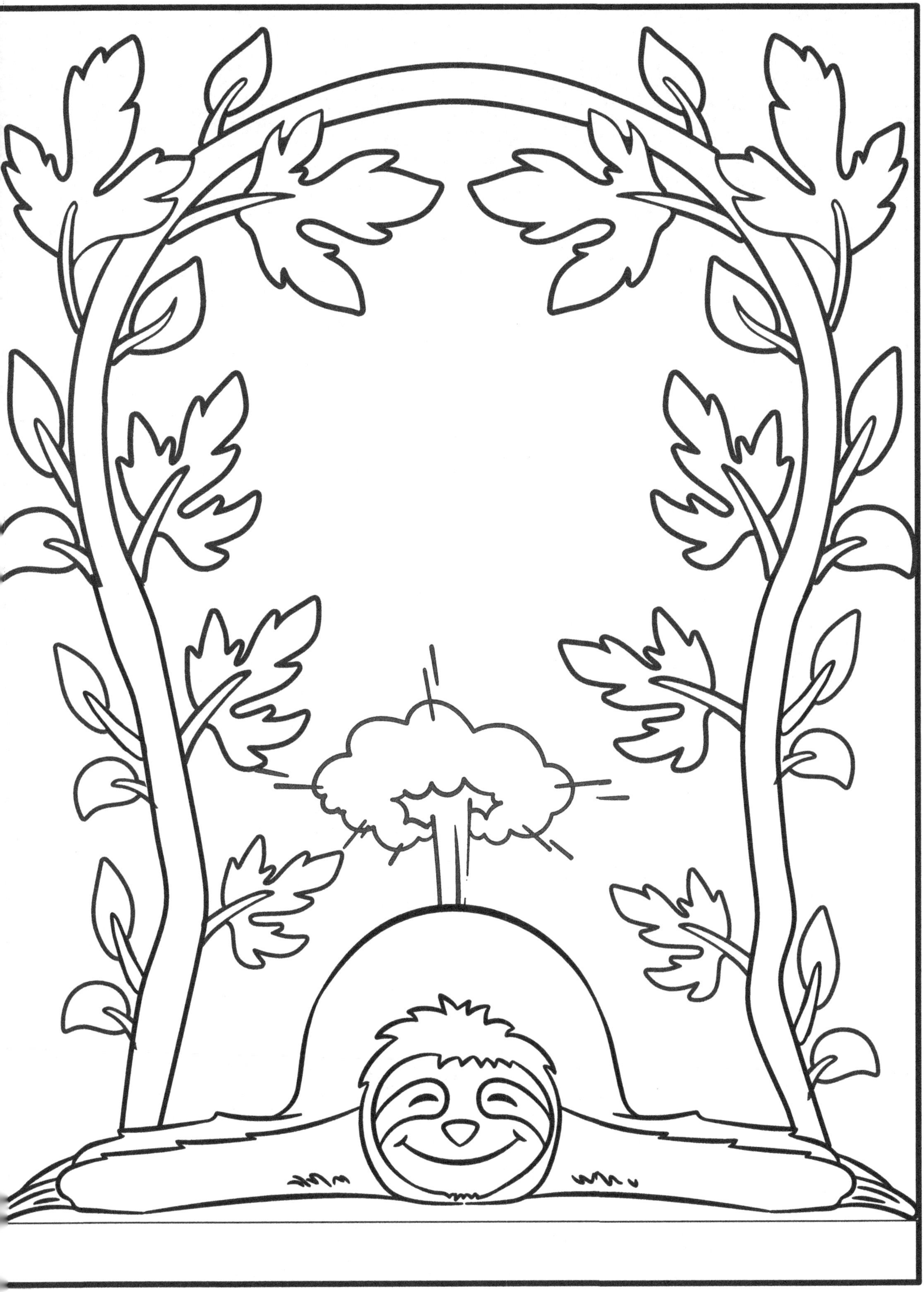

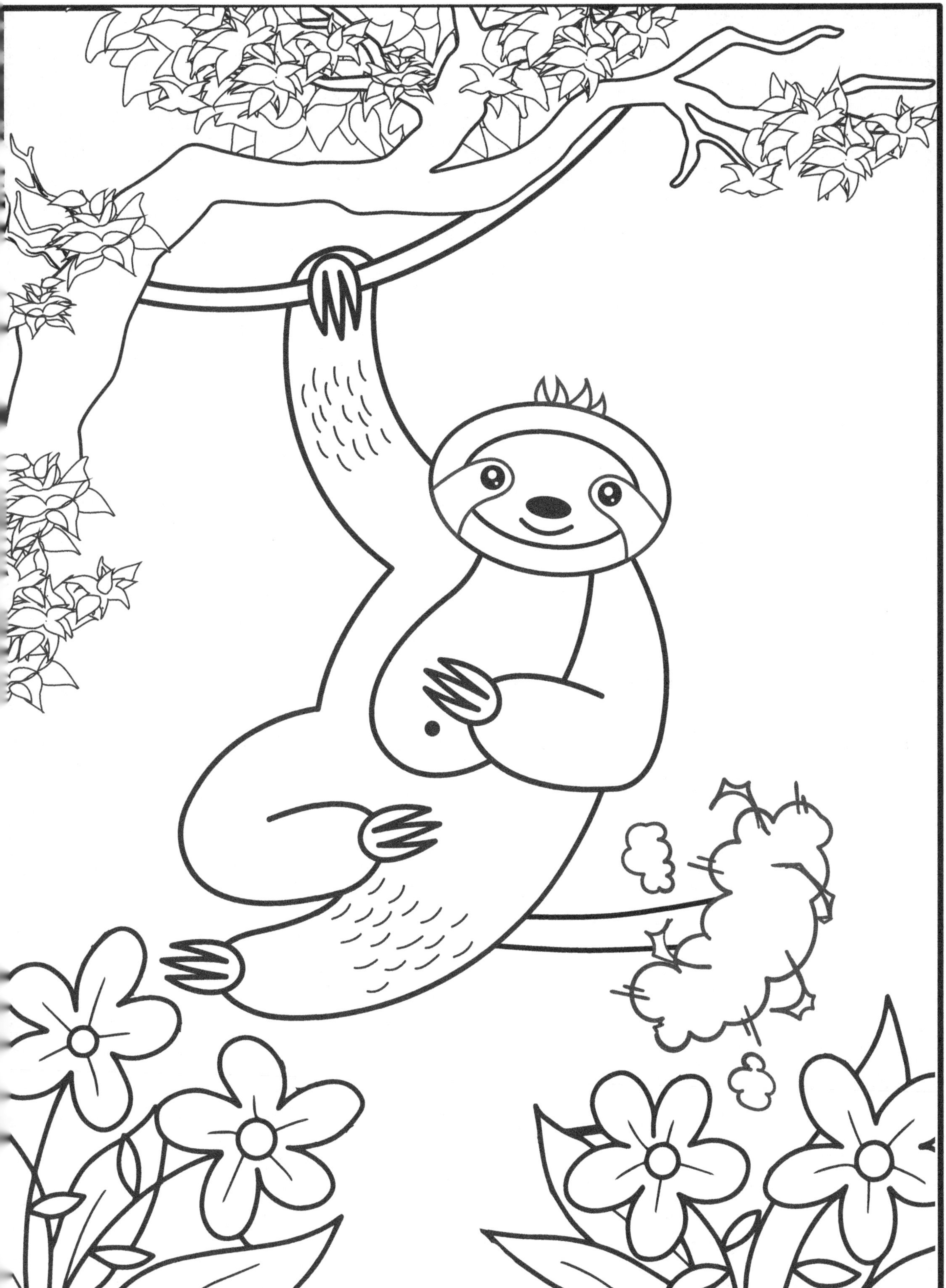

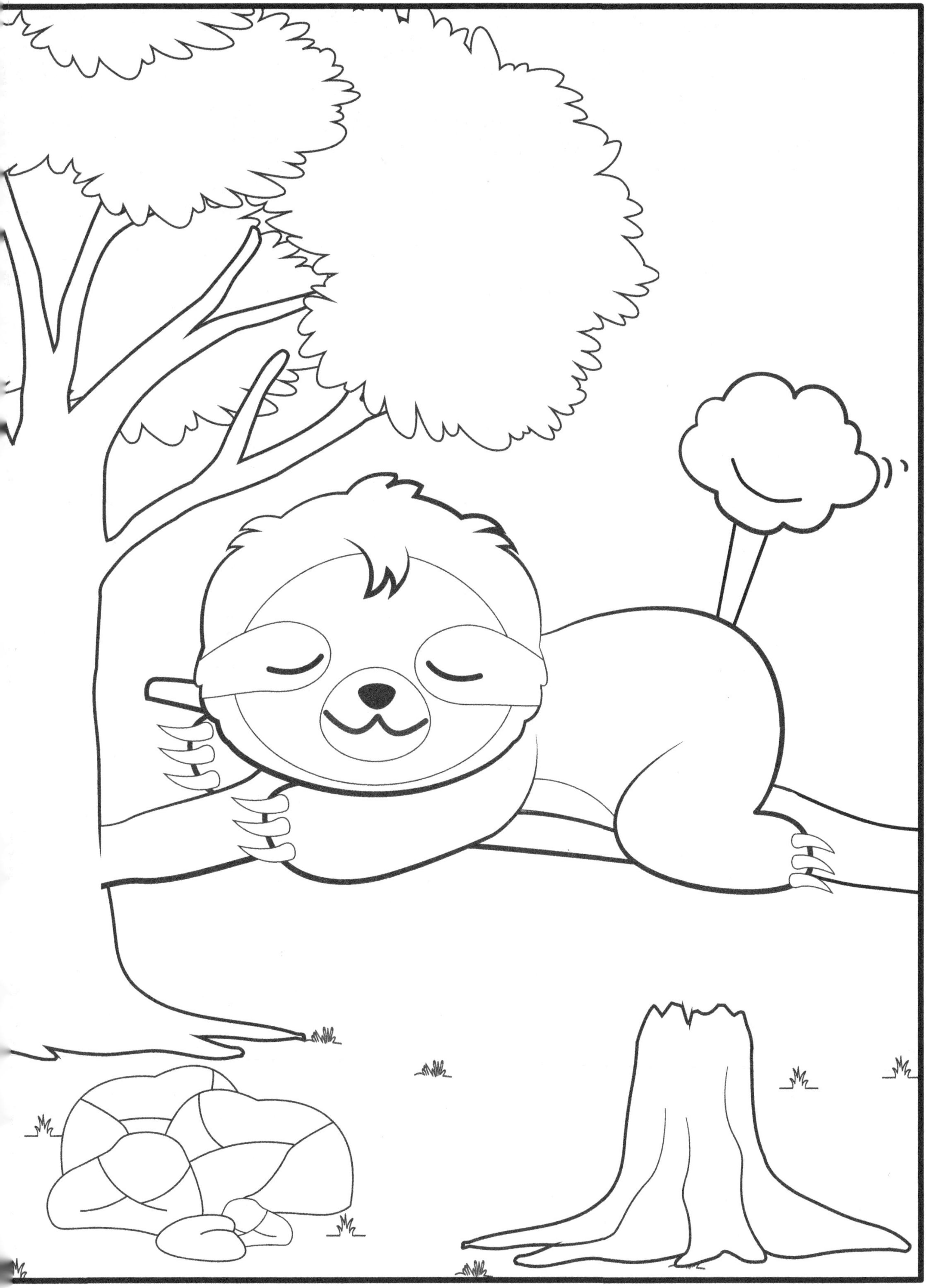

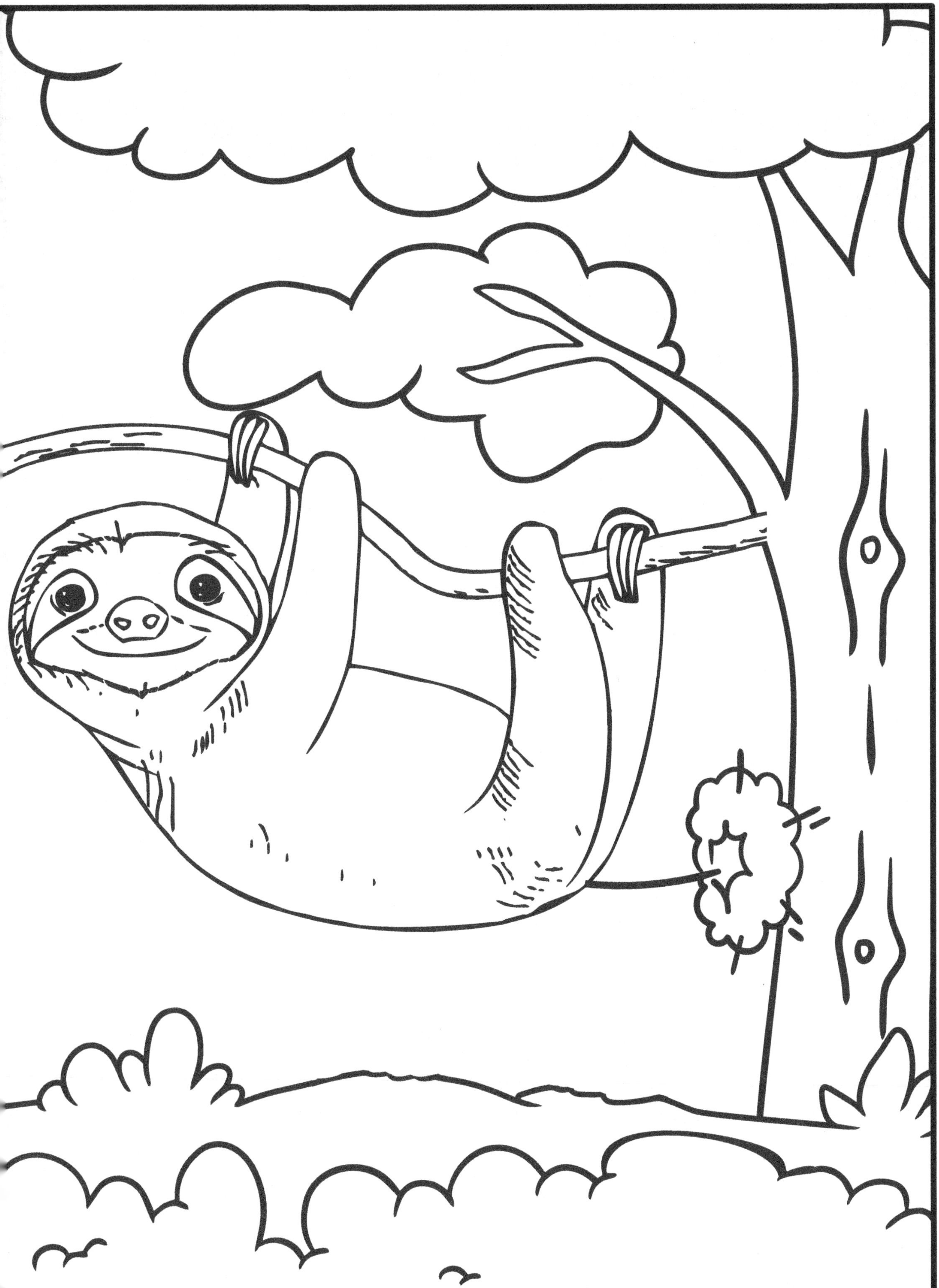

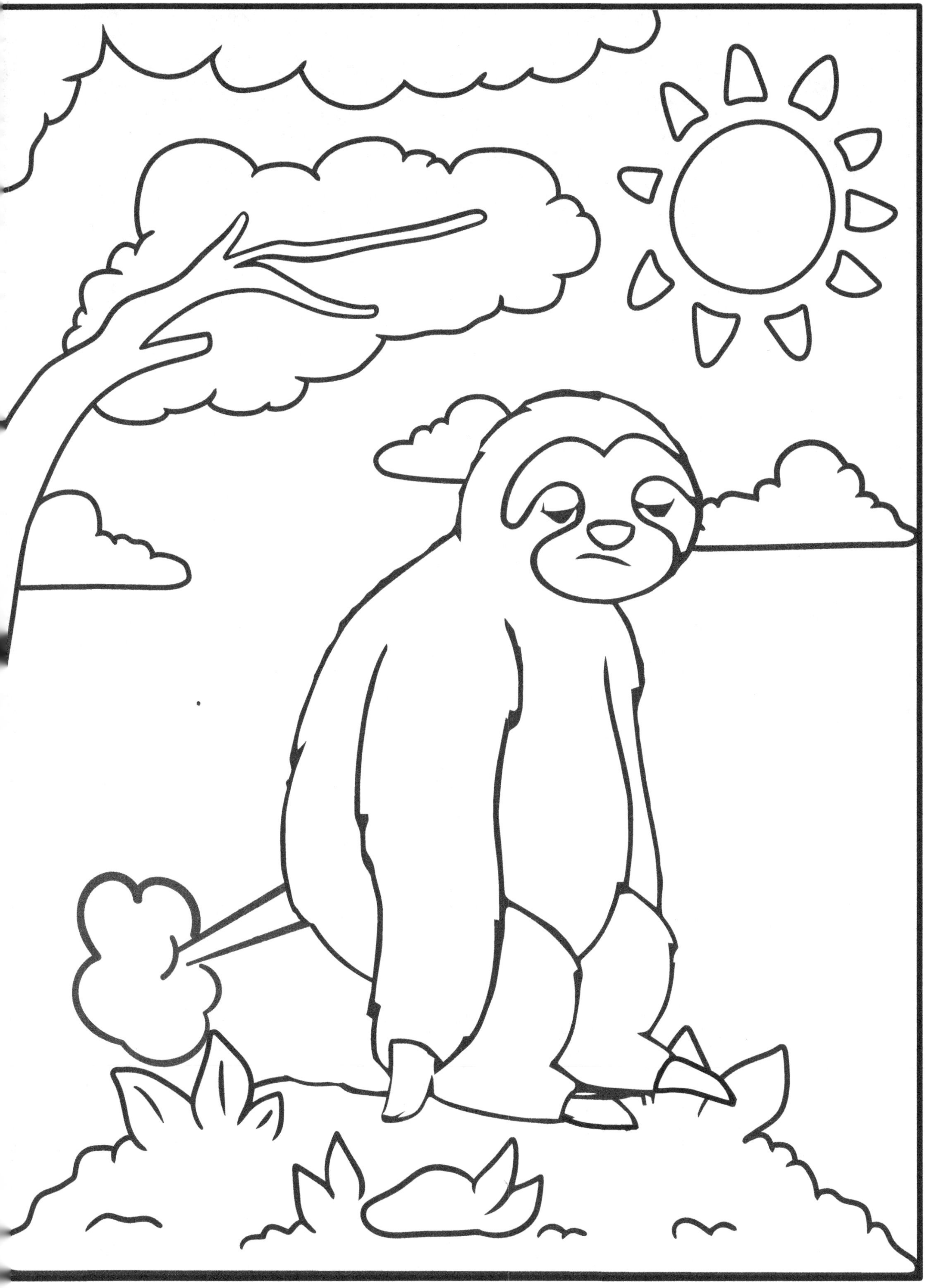

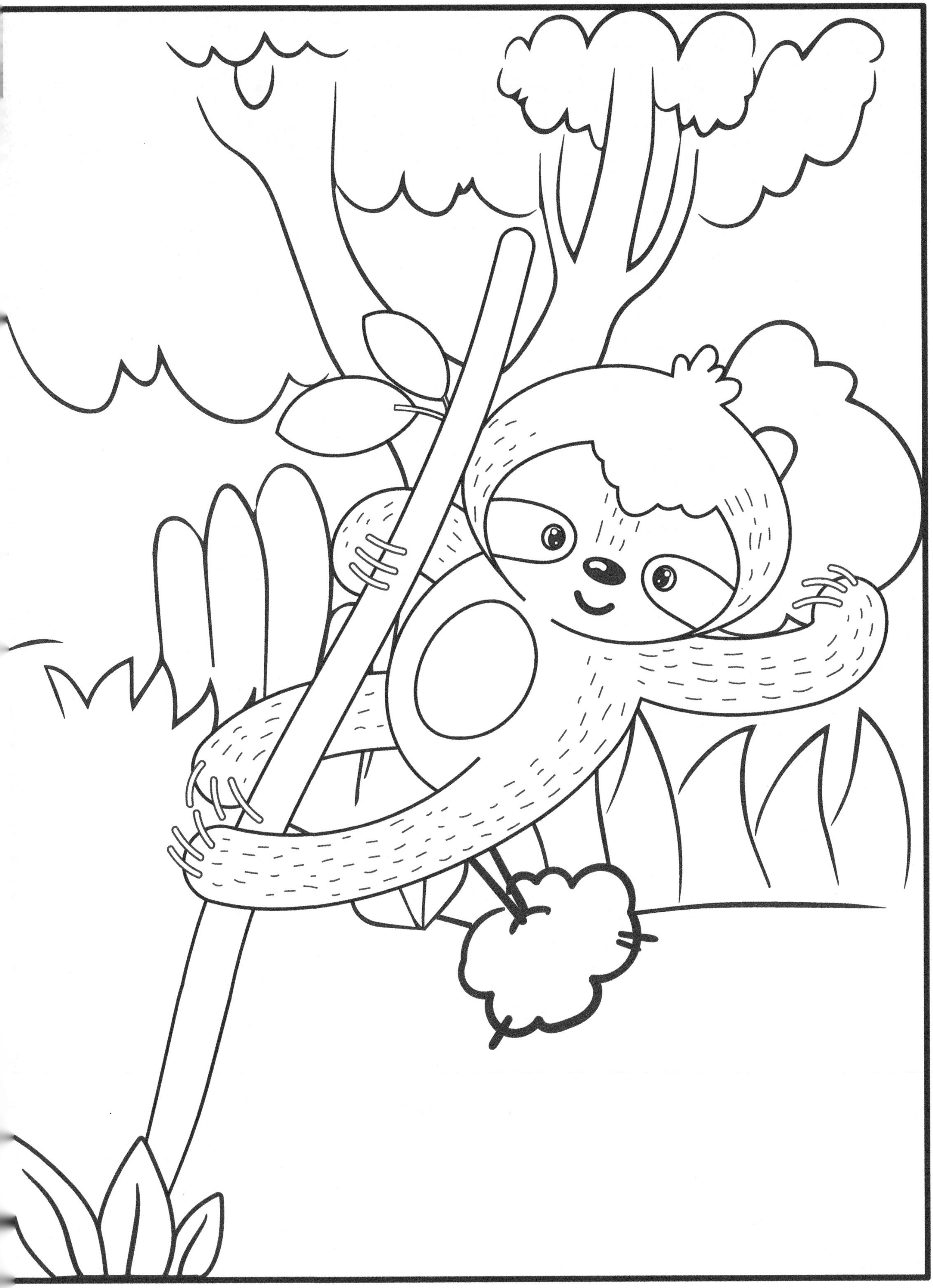

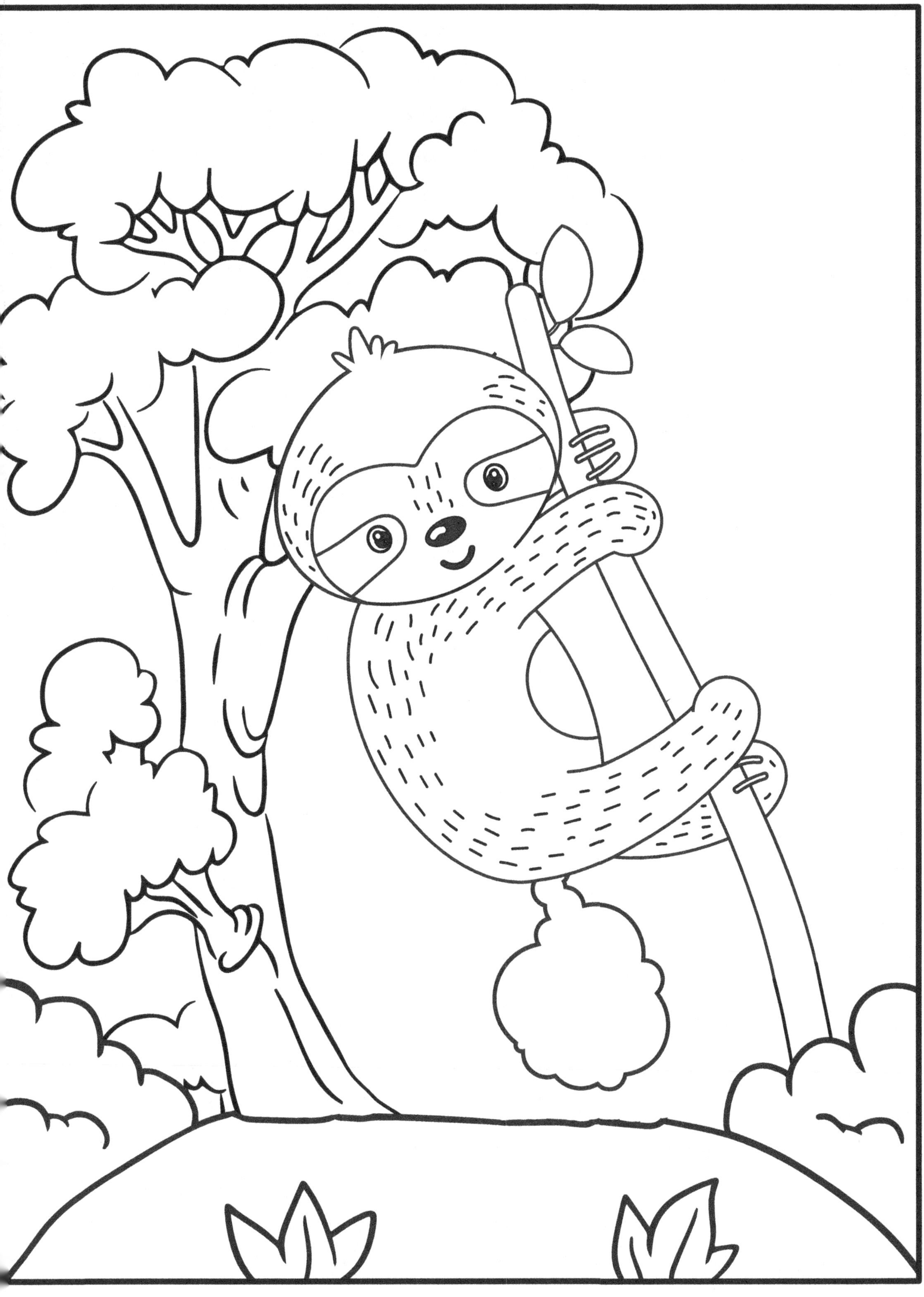

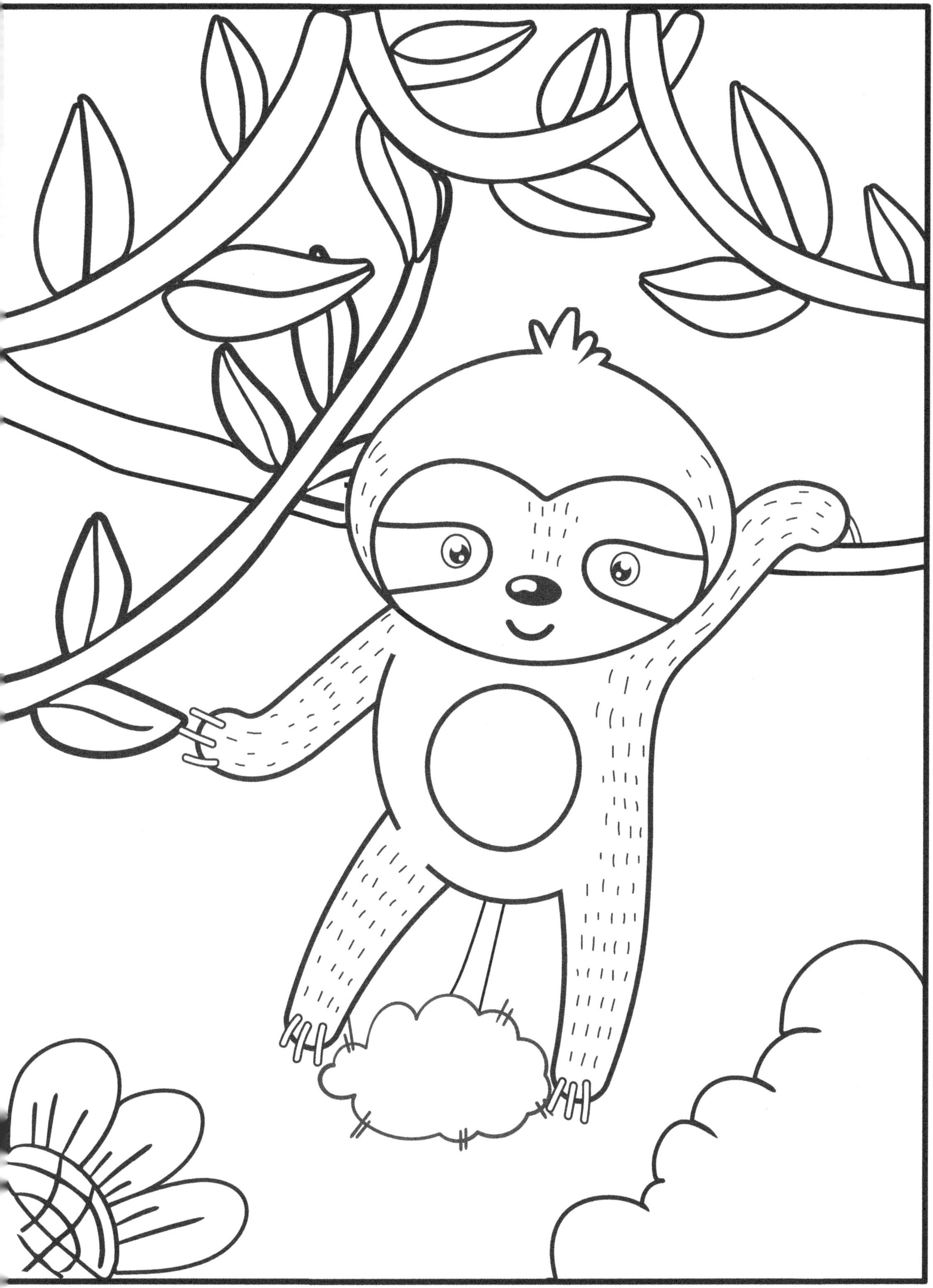

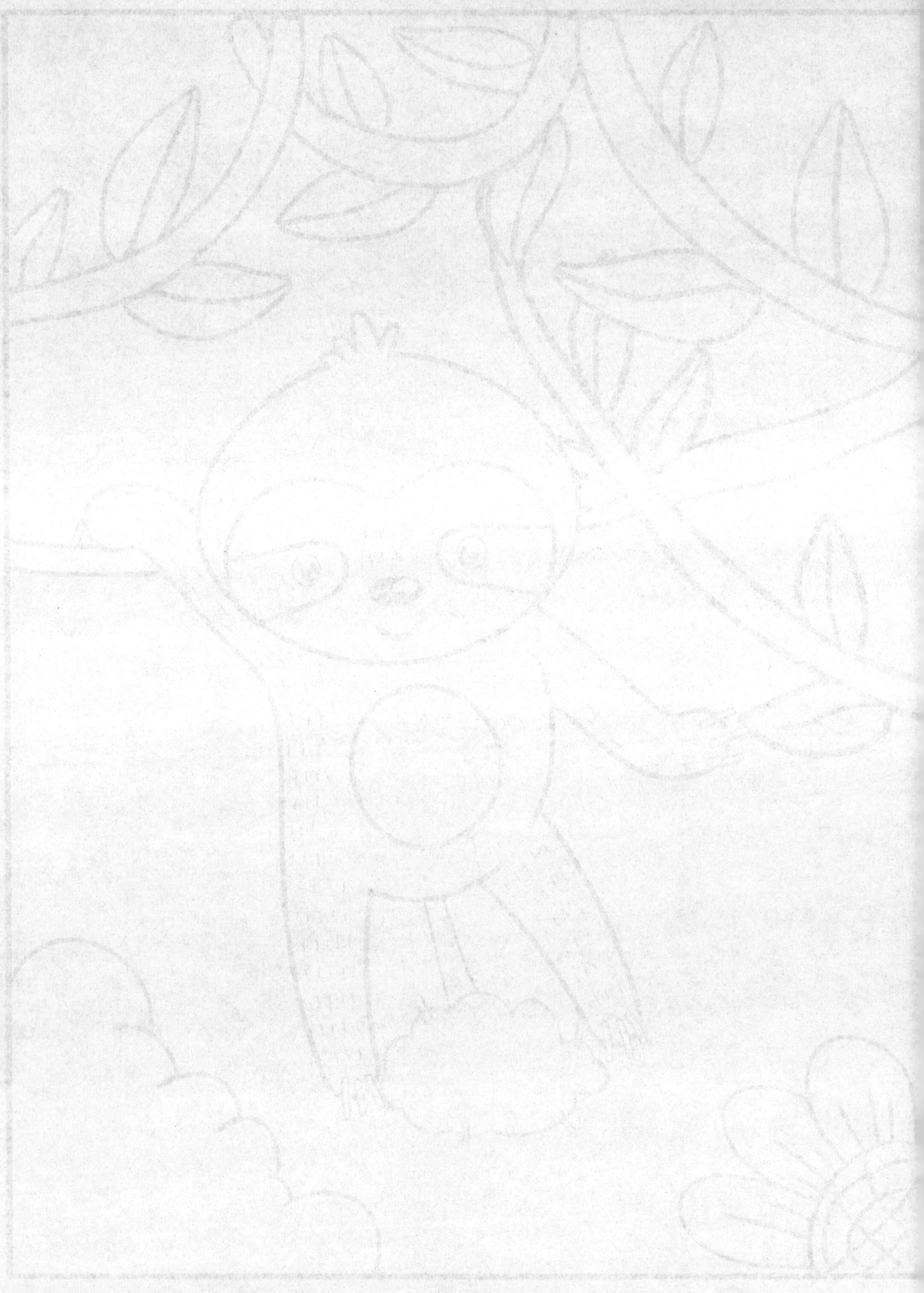

Made in United States
Orlando, FL
17 December 2024

55981684R00037